Beth
Be Yoie

1

RIOT

By
Amy Davies

Copyright

Cover Designer – Designs by Dana
Photographer – Paul Henry Serres Photography
Model – David and Nicholas
Editing – Stephanie Farrant
Formatting – Maria Lazarou @ Obsessed by Books
Designs

Blurb

Nobody expects a dirty mouthed biker to be gay, never mind the Sergeant at Arms of the notorious Road Wreckers MC, but this is the life I lead. The life I love.

I've been keeping them safe, being the defence, and watching them find their Old Ladies, it's left a longing in my heart for him.

That is, until one nightmare of a night brings my decisions back to haunt me. Ben. The boy I kept at arms-length to live his own life, to make his own mistakes, to find his own way.

Will he learn how to let a Riot into his bed and into his heart? Or is almost all we were ever destined to be?

One

Ben

My fingers fly across the keyboard on my laptop. The need to finish this book is driving me bloody crazy. When I get like this, my boyfriend tends to stay clear of me because he knows how much I hate the distractions he throws at me—from walking around half naked to serving the most amazing home-cooked food.

Flexing my fingers, I stretch my back, making it click in multiple places. Fuck me, I'm getting old. Well, not really. I'm only twenty-five, but damn, I feel ninety at times.

Friday, my dog, sighs at my feet, enjoying her nap. Hell, she loves her naps. When I was looking for a dog, I came across her breed, which are rare in the UK, but when I saw her, I had to have her.

My phone dings next to my laptop, and I smile when I see my brother's name road name, because he won't let me use his birth name, Scott on my contacts.

Scott: You doing okay, brother? I know you're finishing up.

I smile at the thought of this crazy-arse fucking biker caring about his baby brother.

Me: Almost done. Two more chapters and the epilogue. I'm good, eating and sleeping. Lol.

Scott: Good. Make sure you take a shit and get laid once in a while, yeah?

Me: Will do, brother of mine. Now piss off. I need to finish.

Scott: Pissing off. Later.

I don't reply. I lock my phone and put it back down on the table, then get back to the story I need to finish. This one has been more mentally challenging than usual, a tad darker and more gruesome.

For someone who hates the sight of blood, I don't half write some gory shit. I was always one to have my head buried in a book in school while my brother shagged his way through every girl who looked his way.

My brother, Mayhem, is a member of the Road Wreckers MC. Actually, he is the VP of the club. They are a scary bunch of guys but will do right by you if you need them.

Pushing my chair back, I get to my feet and make my way to the kitchen, Friday hot on my heels. I need more coffee—strong freaking coffee. While the kettle is boiling, I pull up my social media and scroll through that. I'm not usually one to be on platforms much, but with a new release coming up I tend to keep track of how things are in the book world.

I smile when I see two of my old school friends are getting married and having kids. Good for them. It makes me happy to see people I care about being happy. Kids have never appealed to me. Not because I'm gay but because I just don't feel the need to have them. Though I know Harry does, so I'm not sure what that means for our future.

I have a nephew I love to pieces. Logan is perfect. Biased, I know, but who cares. I can say what I want about him. He makes me smile and forget any shit that is happening in my life. He takes away the stress of my work. Harry finds him annoying at times because, let's be frank, he's a mini-Mayhem.

All I see is a strong little boy who fought the odds, thanks to his junkie bitch of a mother, who left him on my brother's doorstep in the dead of winter.

Speaking of Harry...

Harry: NO work Friday night. We are going out. I am not taking no for an answer.

Shaking my head at his demand, I type out a reply.

Me: Fine. One night, babe. I need to finish this book.

Harry: That book is so fucking important, but can it suck you off like I do?

Me: Don't start. You know you're important to me, but this is my job. I'll talk to you later.

I cut the conversation off because he will bitch for hours if I give him the chance. Picking the kettle up, I make my strong coffee and get back to hitting todays target.

People think that being an author is all fun and games, that we sit on our arses and type out words. They don't see the stress of planning a book, or the editing and the proof reading. Hell, even the cover needs to be perfect. I'm a stickler for making my cover match my story.

Once, Harry found me looking at guys on a photo stock site for a cover and flipped the fuck out, said I was cheating on him. Safe to say, he didn't talk to me for a week.

7

I seem to be stuck in this stagnant relationship with Harry. I know I need to break it off, but I can't seem to make the move. Call me weak, I don't care. He can be so self-centred when he wants to be. Add in some very dramatic flair and he is one big ball of fucked up. Harry is part of a drama company and likes to cause a scene if he thinks it will get him attention.

That's why I'm not surprised to see he hasn't text me back. This is what he does. I have no doubt he will pop by my house and kick off on the front step.

Pushing thoughts of Harry out of my head, I get stuck in, writing as many words as I can. The sooner I finish this book, the quicker I can take a two-week holiday.

I always take some time off between books. It gives me a chance to recharge my brain and get the juices flowing for the next book. I'm a planner when it comes to my stories. I like to know what will happen to my characters.

Again, my fingers fly over the keyboard and my brain goes into story mode, the words flowing. The scene get bloodier, the characters gasp for air and pant with exhaustion. They kiss, they fuck, then they get shot.

Life in some cases, right?

When I published my first book, it was a true story, so to speak. It was lightly based on an experience I had when I was a teenager. I was invited to a party by a guy from the same college as me. He pulled me into the forest and kissed me, and that lead to me giving him a blowjob, but it was all a fucking ploy to beat the shit out of me.

I spent two days in hospital, but lucky for me, I have a brother who is bloody crazy—hence his road name. He and some of his friends, including the man who has been the main character in my many porn-like dreams—Riot, aka Leo Peters—tracked the little shits down and gave them a beating that would leave one of the guys with a permanent limp. Safe to say they stayed clear of me from that night onwards.

For years I have had a crush on Riot, but I know better than to make my crush known. He's a slut and shags any guy who shows him attention. Plus, he's eleven years older than me. Being younger than the guys that hang around my brother was a blessing and a curse. No one would mess with me after that awful night, but it also kept guys from wanting to date me.

It has only been the last few years, since I moved further away, that I've dated. I've had some one-night stands that were enough for me at the time, but then I met Harry and things took a different path. It was worth a try.

He was charming and knew all the right things to say. Plus, he's a stark contrast to the big, burly biker I really want but can never have. Things moved quickly with Harry and I. We went on a few dates then jumped right into bed with each other. He's okay in bed; not the best I've had but he gets me off and me him.

Do I want more? Yes. Of course, I do. But right now, my writing takes precedence in my life, and it's the one thing Harry dislikes so much, because it takes my attention away from him.

My mind wanders to the lead character in my current book. He kind of reminds me of Riot. All tall, dark, and very handsome, with his dark hair, his dark stubble, and muscles for days. He's only a few inches taller than me, but he still makes me feel small on a good day.

There have been times over the years when I've seen Riot looking at me, but he just winks and turns way. He never acts on whatever he's thinking. Sometimes I can feel the pull between us, but again, nothing ever gets done. Even though I have never told anyone of my crush for Riot, I have no doubt that he and some of the brothers have some sort of inkling about what I feel for him.

My mum, Babs, knows. Hell, she often tells me that I should just tell Riot how I feel because life is too damned short to fuck it up and waste it on fairy boys like Harry—her words, not mine. When my parents and brother met Harry, they made it known to me the first chance they got that I needed to end it, because he was a dick and not worth my time. But back then, there was the possibility of settling with someone who actually wanted to settle down, to be in a committed relationship.

Knowing what I know about Riot, it's obvious he will never settle down. He likes to fuck way too much to stick to fucking one arse for the rest of his life. That's why I stay clear of him. Yeah, I go to club parties and family events, but mostly I stay away. I know my heart and soul couldn't take actually seeing him be with someone else; touching them, kissing them, and eventually hearing him shag them in his room.

One time, when I popped in to pick up Logan, Riot was getting his dick sucked by some guy who was known around town for getting on his knees for anyone who asked. They were down the side of the building. Riot saw me, and I froze on the spot, expecting him to stop, but he didn't. He kept fucking the guy's mouth while keeping his gaze locked on mine.

Lord knows how long I stood there for, but as he was coming down the guy's throat, I swear to everything holy he muttered my name. Then, in a flash, he was tucking himself away, winking at me, and walking away.

After that, I stayed away for weeks, unable to look Riot in the eye. I never told Mayhem why I wasn't coming around. I just made excuses. That worked for all of six weeks, then a member of the club hit a milestone birthday and I was dragged to the clubhouse by my parents. I avoided Riot as much as possible, but with his huge body, he seemed to be everywhere I looked.

We didn't speak, but I didn't miss the narrowed eyes and the thin lips when Harry arrived. They have made their dislike for him clear, and to be completely honest, I've been thinking a lot lately as to why I'm still with him.

My phone rings, the ringtone revealing it's my mother calling me. Groaning, I close my eyes, then pick up my phone and answer it.

"Hey, Mum," I greet.

"Ben? Ben, can you hear me? Damned these stupid phones with no buttons. I don't have the foggiest if it works or not. Damn, Leon, I think it's broken," she fusses into the phone at my dad, and I have to hold back my laughter at her.

My mum doesn't like technology changing at all.

"Mum, I can hear you."

"Oh, Ben. I thought this stupid thing was broken," she huffs.

God, I love my mum. She is a firecracker on steroids. She literally has no filter, and she doesn't care what she says or to whom she says it. She says what she means and means what she says. Let's just say that some people get offended by what she has to say, but she does mean it in the kindest of ways.

"It works fine, Mum. What did you call for?"

"Have you finished the book? I want to take you out for a nice meal when you do. You know, to celebrate."

I smile at her offer. Both my parents are proud of what I have achieved and support everything I do. They even support everything Mayhem does. Even when things were hard at times with Logan, they were right there with him.

When I told them I was gay, I wasn't sure what to expect, but my mum cried, and my dad hugged me. Then my mum threw herself at me and cried even more, saying she was so happy that I finally told her.

We are lucky in the parents department.

"That would be nice, Mum. I'm almost done. Maybe another day or two. Then we can go to that little place you like, with the outside area."

"Oh, that would be lovely, Benny."

We chat for a little while longer, then we hang up and I get back to work, writing as many words down as I can before relaxing for the rest of the day.

Two

Riot

My fingers knot in the guy's long hair. It's not something I usually go for, but fuck me, his lips looked good and I just knew he would be a champ at sucking cock.

"Fuck," I grind out through clenched teeth. He's sucking my dick like a damned hoover on a power trip.

Not many people can take my whole length, but this fucker is giving it the good old college try. Suddenly, he gags, and the sound spurs me on. I press his head down, making him choke on me.

His head snaps back and he glares up at me, but I just smirk at him. This is what you get when you want to get down and dirty with a biker. You don't get nice, sweet, and gentle. You get hard, dirty, and fucking rough.

"What the fuck, Riot?" he bitches, making me chuckle.

"Hey, you wanted to suck my cock. I'm happy to find another bloke willing to do the job for me. No skin off my nose." I shrug and go to get to my feet, but his hands find my thighs and hold me in place. "Yeah, thought so. Get back to it." I push his head back down until his mouth swallows my dick again.

I adjust myself on the hard chair to get more comfortable, which forces my dick to the back of his throat, making him gag. The gay bar I'm at is one I go to when I want to get off, or I call one of my regulars to come round to the club. Not many gay men come to the club to hang around like the bitches do.

"Fuck yeah, take it, bitch." My lips thin as my hips rock, and my balls tighten.

Without warning him, I come, shooting my load into his mouth, not caring if he takes it all or chokes on it. He makes gagging sounds, and his heavy breathing brings a smile to my face. I hold his head for a few seconds longer before I finally let him go. He falls back onto his arse, wiping his mouth with the back of his hand as he glares at me.

"What?" I ask, tucking my still hard dick away.

I get to my feet and walk over to the small kitchen that's in the private rooms at the club. Pulling open the fridge, I take out a beer, not bothering to ask if he wants one or not.

"What the fuck was that? I couldn't breathe when you held me down." I turn to face the grumpy fuck, who really should be fucking honoured to have sucked my dick.

"That was me getting my dick sucked, and now I'm having a beer before getting the fuck out of here. I have shit to do." I shrug and down the bottle, then dump it on the counter.

"So, just like that, you're going to come and leave? What about me?" he whines. I can see his anger building, but all that does is make me chuckle.

"What about you? I'm sure your hands work just fucking fine. Get yourself off. I never came here for that shit. Besides, you did a mediocre job at best."

I walk towards the door, pulling my phone out of my pocket to see if Prez has text me the information for the next shipment.

"That's a shitty thing to do, Riot. Lose my number," he bitches. I shake my phone at him and laugh.

"I don't have your number, fuckface." With that, I make my exit and head to my bike.

A gay man in a motorcycle club isn't something you see often, but the Road Wreckers MC don't give a shit who you fuck. As long as your dick doesn't get in the way of club business, or bring drama to the club, they're good with whatever. I live by three rules: never fuck a guy more than once; never bring trouble to the club; and *never* let a guy top me.

I'm the top.

Seeing fuck all from Chaos, I get on my bike and head to the clubhouse. The guy may have sucked me off and made me come, but the tension in my shoulders is still tight as fuck.

Before I left, I heard Mayhem talking on the phone to his mum, Babs. They spoke about his brother, Ben, finishing his book, and how his so-called fucking boyfriend isn't being supportive and is instead whining all the time.

Ben is a fucking wicked guy. He's handsome as fuck, and while he can be shy at times, he's fierce when he needs to be, something I respect. That man works hard as fuck to get his books written, and I have read every motherfucking one of them. Not that anyone fucking knows, because they would rip the shit out of me.

I've had my eye on Ben for years, but with him being Mayhem's little brother, I've kept my distance—not that I haven't enjoyed toying with him. The day he came out as gay was a fucking joyous day for me, let me tell you. But in true Riot style, I went and fucked a bloke so hard he was unable to walk out of the hotel room, because I knew that even though he was gay, he was off limits to me, and that fucked with my head.

He always gave off the vibe of being gay, but people waited until he was ready to come out of the closet. Then, not long after he came out, he was involved in a shitty incident, during which he got the hell beat out of him. When we found out, me, Mayhem, and the brothers dealt with the fucks who hurt him. Since that day, I have always kept him in my sights, but did nothing to let him know I was interested. He was always Mayhem's little brother in my head, and my dick didn't appreciate that.

Years of knowing he's had a crush on me has always done something to me. Does he think of me when his boyfriend fucks him or sucks him off? Does he wish it were me and not him?

These questions will be answered someday, but not any time soon. By the looks of things, Ben and his man look semi-happy.

Until then, I will bed my way through the Eastford gay men who want to fuck a dirty biker.

My bike carries me through the town streets that are filled with people enjoying their Friday night drinking. No doubt they'll soon be getting a kebab or burger before heading home.

I gun the throttle, making my baby purr between my legs as I race beneath the streetlights that illuminate the wet road—got to love summer in Britain—and the black and chrome of my Harley. I smile. This baby is my girl, not only because she's stunning but because I built her from scratch and did the custom paint job.

Working with vehicles is one of the many things I do for the club. I handle the garage and am responsible for getting our transport vehicles ready for shipment. We ship drugs all over the UK and to some European cites. We use cars, bikes, buses, and even boats to get our product out to our clients.

The club only deals in drugs. We don't touch guns—well, unless we need to use them. The club earns enough from the drugs and the bar in the clubhouse. There are plenty of fuckers who want to come round to hang with a biker, and many bitches who want to fuck a biker—well, except me.

When I tell them I'm not interested in the pussy and tits they have, they start off shocked but soon get pissed. Maybe it's because they see me as competition. I mean, I am one sexy motherfucker.

When I pull up at the clubhouse, the prospect pulls the tall wire gate open and gives me a chin lift as I pass through. He's a good kid. He knows his place and understands the importance of respect.

After parking my bike next to my brothers', I kill the engine and pull my helmet off, resting it on my seat before walking into the clubhouse. The music is the first thing to hit me, then the smoke-filled air and scent of beer, and I fucking love it. It's the smell of home.

I see my brothers sitting around with their old ladies on their laps. It's something that has always made me chuckle, because can you image me chilling with them with some guy on my lap? Yeah, that shit would look weird as fuck. Though if I did have a man, I would keep him close.

"Riot, I see you managed to dislodge your cock from the guy's arse long enough to grace us with your presence," Chaos calls out to me.

I smirk and flip the fucker off, then walk over to them, signalling to the prospect behind the bar to bring me a whisky.

My back creaks as I settle down in one of the empty chairs. Fuck me, I'm getting old. Even though I'm only thirty-six, some days I feel like I'm eighty. Every joint clicks from being under the hood of a car, or under a boat.

"I didn't fuck the little shit, but his mouth was pretty wicked." I wiggle my eyebrows.

My brothers laugh, Lizzie shakes her head, and Olivia and Evie just smile at me. They all know my antics. I don't ever shy away from being gay. It's who I am.

Don't like it then you can fuck off, simple as that.

"How's the four-by-four coming along?" Mayhem asks.

17

"Good. Almost done. It was a pain in the fucking arse getting the under panel off, but it eventually shifted. It should be finished tomorrow, ready for the next shipment."

"Good. I need everything to run smoothly with this one. They wanted more this time, so more money for us. This is good for the club. We pull this shit off and it opens up a whole new path for us."

We all nod because what Mayhem is saying is true. We started with small cars and boats, now we use larger cars, buses, and large yachts that carry high-end rich fuckers who have no clue we're storing drugs on the boat they hired.

I yawn, making the guys laugh at me.

"Yeah, yeah, I know, fuckers. I may be getting old, but so are you bastards. I'm out. I need my beauty sleep."

Stepping over to my brothers, I fist bump them then kiss their women on the cheek. A bunch of 'good nights' are exchanged before I head to my room at the back of the club.

Once inside, I quickly strip my clothes off and get into to bed, then lie there with my eyes closed to re-hash the day. Today could have been shit, what with the cars and the fucker I hooked up with, but it ended up being okay.

My life is chaotic and filled with risk, so I live each day as if it is my last.

Tomorrow is a new day. Be happy that you get another chance at it.

Three

Ben

Music is pounding through the speakers of the club, and it's so not to my taste. I would rather hear old-school rock and some old chart music. I hate all this techno shit.

I do not want to fucking be here, but I promised Harry I would come.

Throwing back the shot the bartender just placed in front of me, I turn and look at the dancefloor, where my current boyfriend is grinding his arse on some stranger. This is what he always does. When we fight, he drinks like a fish and then pulls shit like this to make me jealous, but it's wearing thin on me right now.

"Man, he is all over him tonight," Dan says from my side, and I nod to my childhood friend.

"Yeah. He's pissed at me."

"What a fucking surprise. Ben, you need to dump his arse," he tells me.

I know he's right, but I feel comfortable around Harry—sometimes—so I think that's why I stick around—that and the fact I can't have the one man I want.

"Why is he pissed this time?"

"I need to finish my book; my deadline is soon."

"Doesn't that man know you get paid for your work while he prances around on a fucking stage for nothing?"

"He doesn't care, Dan. I think it's time to be honest." I shake my head. What a bloody waste of three years.

"Lose the deadweight, Benny Boy," he replies, and I smile at his use of the nickname my brother gave me. Mayhem may be a hard as hell biker, but when it comes to his family, he loves fiercely.

"Fuck me," I growl when I see Harry twerking like he's some teenage girl.

Everyone cheers him on, and he laps up the attention, doing more provocative moves.

I'm sick of his antics. Maybe it is time to call it a day with him.

The bloke he's dancing with cups his jaw and turns Harry's head like he's going to kiss him, and Harry fucking lets him.

My blood boils, but not with jealousy, which is strange. What the hell bothers me is the fact our friends are here, and they know we are together. He's disrespecting me in front of everyone.

Slamming the glass down, I march across the room and pull Harry from his dance partner, who pushes my chest.

"Back off, mate. I saw him first," he snaps.

"No, mate. He's my boyfriend, and he's pushing my buttons." I glare at Harry, who smirks drunkenly at me. "Are you seriously enjoying this right now?" I grind out, and Harry shrugs, keeping the smirk in place.

"Well maybe you should have been dancing with your man, so he wouldn't come looking for someone else."

"Fuck off," I snap. It takes a lot for me to snap at people. I'm usually the calm one who will stand back and people watch, but tonight, a whole new range of buttons have been pushed.

I notice that some people have stopped dancing and are watching the scene play out.

"It was only dancing, Ben. No need to get your knickers in a twist," Harry states, and it pisses me the hell off.

"It wasn't only dancing, Harry. You are always pulling this shit." I huff, and he smiles, stepping closer and resting a hand on my chest.

"But I like it when you're jealous. It shows you care." Is he for fucking real?

"Care? Of course I fucking care for you, Harry. Don't you care about me?" I reply.

"No, you always care about those stupid books you write. They take up all your time. I don't get to see you," he whines, clearly thinking he's being cute right now, but bloody hell, he looks like a whiney little toddler.

"Stupid books? Take up all my time? You're at dance and drama most of the fucking week, Harry. I barely see you. And you have the fucking cheek to tell me that my job, a job that *actually* fucking pays my bills, is stupid and a joke?" I breathe heavily, pinching the bridge of my nose.

Opening my eyes, I look him square on. "You need to think about what the hell you want. I'm going." I spin on my heel and leave, not bothering to wait for a reply.

Pushing through the throng of partygoers, I make it outside. The British air is just starting to turn a little chilly and I shiver. Shaking my head, trying to clear the thoughts, I start walking down the street, making my way to the taxi rank to get a ride home.

"Ben, wait." I turn around to see Harry running after me, but I don't stop. "For crying out loud, Ben. Stop."

I do, keeping my back to him and waiting for him to catch up with me. He moves to stand in front of me, huffing and puffing from the very short distance he just jogged. He may do dance and drama, but he is really unfit, which is why he

21

lies there in bed and I do all the work. Another red flag I skipped over I suppose.

"Say what you have to say, because I want to go home and cool off before we both say something one of us will regret," I tell him. He narrows his eyes at me.

"You need to lighten the hell up, Ben. You should feel lucky I'm with you. Most men would be happy to be with me, but you… all you do is take it for granted." He huffs, crossing his arms and popping a hip. Ever the drama queen.

"Then why are you with me, Harry?" I reply, shaking my head, not really wanting to do this shit here. "Do you know what, I don't want to know. Just go back to your friends and do whatever the hell you want, because you're doing that anyway."

He goes to speak but a voice slices through the night. A cold wash rushes through me, while Harry's face goes ghost-white and his body locks up with fear.

"Look what we have here, boys. Two fucking faggots," someone says from behind me.

Instead of looking back, I keep my head up and move closer to the taxi. A shiver runs down my spine because I know this situation only has two outcomes: they leave me alone, or they don't. I'm hoping for the former.

"You a deaf faggot, fuck face?" gets called. I can hear the amusement in their voice.

Looking over my shoulder, I see three guys walking toward us, all decked out in joggers and hoodies. They seem to have an air about them, like they enjoy making trouble, and tonight, we are their targets.

"Not deaf. I just refuse to respond to ignorance," I reply. Harry's eyes widen in fear and shock because usually I'm not one to confront people, but tonight, he has pushed me enough, and the alcohol is helping my bravado.

"Oh, so he has a big mouth. I bet he loves sucking cock like the faggot he is," one chimes in.

22

"How original. Yes, we are gay. Do you have a problem with that?" I ask, folding my arms over my chest.

"Shut up," Harry whispers, fear evident in his voice.

"No, Harry. For fuck's sake grow a pair, will you. No one gives a shit if people are gay anymore. They just get on with their lives. Why should I, or any other gay person out there, take this bullshit from people? We should be able to live our lives like anyone else. We all eat, sleep, and breathe the same way; we just shag a little differently.

"That's the problem with society right now. They're scared of a little change. Well, grow the fuck up. The time to live is now. Be you and fuck everyone else. We are not mentally or physically hurting anyone. People need to get over it," I snap at Harry, but I see the three men stepping close and looking pissed as fuck.

"It is fucking wrong, man. It's sick. You're a fucking pervert," one snaps, and I can't stop the humourless laugh that breaks free. Harry gasps and steps behind me. Pussy.

"I am sick of this shit. There is nothing wrong with being gay. It's just who we are," I grind out to them and puff out my chest. I'm taller than two of the men, but I know there is no way I can take all three on at once.

Mayhem has always made sure I stayed fit and could handle myself in a one-on-one situation, but three on one... I'm fucked if they attack. And the feeling I'm getting right now says they are seconds away from doing just that.

"Nah, man. Men are made for fucking bitches. I think we need to teach you a fucking lesson for mouthing off."

"Yeah, I'm sure he just winked at me, the fucking perve," one adds.

"Oh, come on. That old chestnut is old as fuck. Just leave."

Fucking typical of society these days—always making something out to be what it's not. Putting their own spin on things to make trouble and ruin people lives. Just remember that there are always two sides to every story you hear and read.

This is why the media is toxic and likes to stir shit up, making you think what they want you to think. They plant the seed, and you water it, and it festers into something that may not be true, but they want you to think it is so you attack.

They don't waste a second as they all lunge for me. I throw jabs, as they punch and kick at me. I use the techniques Mayhem and Psycho taught me, and get a few hits in, catching one in the eyes. He screams like a little girl, before his anger spikes. One comes at me from behind, and I bend at the waist and flip him over, making him land heavily on the concrete. But the other two use that time to come at me.

They manage to get me to the ground, adding kick after kick, hitting all over my body. I cry out when one stamps on my hand, my fingers instantly curling into a fist. Forcing my eyes open, I catch a small glimpse of Harry running way.

Fucking cunt.

I cry out as the hits keep coming, until someone yells at them to leave me alone. Then the hits stop. Hands touch me, checking my pulse, as I moan in pain. My body aches and feels like it's on fire.

"Keep still, man. Someone has called the police," a man says.

"Road Wreckers MC. Take me there, please."

"What? The MC? Man, you need to stay clear of them."

I instantly regret it when I shake my head. Pain rattles through my brain as I vomit all over the pavement.

"MC, please. Brother."

"Did he just say his brother is in the MC?" someone else asks.

"Yeah. He did. Fuck, man, we had better get him to the clubhouse. I know how fucking crazy those bastards are."

24

Someone lifts me, and I cry out in pain. Every part of my body feels like it's being ripped in different directions. The pain distracts me from my surroundings, and before I know it, I can hear voices again.

"What the fuck happened?" Mayhem. I sigh when I hear my brother's voice.

"We found him outside a club. Three guys were beating the fuck out of him. We chased them away and tried calling for an ambulance, but he asked us to bring him here, so we did."

"Ben, can you hear me, brother?"

I nod at Mayhem, and he sighs.

"Let's get him inside and into the medic room."

This time, I'm lifted by a pair of thick, strong arms. His scent invades my senses, and I relax, so much so that I moan at the extra pain it causes me.

Riot. His name bounces around my fuzzy head.

Shit. Why does he get to see me at my worst? Bloody hell. He's going to think I'm a wuss, someone who can't fight when needed. Riot likes his men strong, like him. A man who can handle the pounding he gives them—his words, not mine.

When it comes to Riot and me, there isn't much difference except the age gap. I'm a fraction shorter than him, and he packs a bit more muscle and weight than me, but that's it. Add in the fact that he has a light sprinkling of hair on his chest that flows down to his six-pack, continuing into a sexy trail that leads into the waistband of his jeans, and he is sex on a stick. Whereas I'm completely smooth all over, except for my hair and my short beard.

"Breathe, Ben," is all he says as he lays me down on a bed that smells like him.

"Now is not the time, Riot. Move him to the medic room," I hear Chaos rumble.

"Not happening, brother. He needs a comfortable place to rest up and the beds in there are hard as fuck. He stays."

My body sinks into the mattress, and everything goes black as a hand smooths my hair back.

Four

Riot

Fuck me running. Ben looks like he went twenty rounds with Connor McGregor, Anthony Joshua, and Joe Calzaghe all in one fight. His face is covered in blood and bruises.

His body is just as bad. Me and Mayhem stripped him down to his boxers, and I have to say that even with the bruises forming on his body, my cock twitched in my jeans. Sick, I know, to see this man unconscious and getting a fucking hard-on, but hell, Ben is one sexy bastard on a good day.

Mayhem has known for years that I had a thing for Ben, but he threatened me to not make a move until I knew I could give him my all.

Seeing my club brothers settle down over the last few months has made me see how things can be for me. When I worked out that I was gay, my fucked-up parents told me I was a degenerate and that I had to leave their house. I never thought I would have a family until I came across the club, and thank fuck I did. They are my family, deep in my soul, and Ben is a part of that family.

Don't get me wrong, I'm a fucking arsehole to some of the people I fuck, but I'm a biker, so what do they expect. I live by my rules and the club laws.

27

When the prospect came running into the clubhouse screaming about some guys having a beaten brother in the car, I never thought it would be Ben. I thought it might be one of my other brothers, because Keys was out shagging the new bird he has been hooking up with this last month, and he was the only fucker not here.

When we got to the car, it was inside the compound because the prospect recognised Ben and let them through.

Mayhem pulled the door open and cursed up a storm when he saw the state of Ben. Then he went into overdrive and grilled the guys who drove him here, but they stood their ground and told us what happened.

I pushed past him and lifted Ben into my arms, then carried him to my room, ignoring the protests from Chaos and Mayhem about putting him in the medic room. That room is set up like a fucking Grade A hospital, with top notch equipment, but the beds are shit, so I put him in my room.

I also think it was a conscious thing to have him close to me. Though Ben will not be pleased that I have seen him like this. He will think that I see him as weak, but I don't. Ben is a strong man, with self-respect and strong morals. But he thinks people look down on him because he's gay and an author of some of the best fucking books out there right now.

It has been three hours since Ben was brought here. The club's doc came in and cleaned him up. He had to stitch one of the two gashes on the side of his head and add butterfly stitches to the other cuts he got on his face and neck. He's also got two broken fingers but no internal bleeding, and that is it, thank fuck.

The boys have been by to check on him, but they haven't stayed long because I know they are out looking for who did this to him.

A knock on my bedroom door sounds again.

"Come in," I say but don't look to the door, my gaze fixed on the man lying in my bed.

"How is he?" comes Mayhem's voice as the door opens. "Still no change?"

Finally looking up from the chair I'm sitting on, I sigh and shrug.

"Nah, the same. He twitches now and then but sleeps mostly."

He nods but says nothing else. We stay like that for some minutes, neither of us saying anything, just thinking of what the hell happened and where to go from here.

"Any news on the fuckers who did this?"

"Yeah. A street cam caught the whole thing. The little shits came out of nowhere and just started on Ben."

"They? There was more than one?"

"Yeah. The bloke who drove him here said it looked like there were three, but the footage confirmed it. He fought back though. Did real fucking good." I can hear the pride in Mayhem's voice when explaining that Ben fought back.

"Fucking hell. I'm glad he got a few licks in." I sigh and run my fingers through my short hair.

"Any ID's?" Mayhem shakes his head at my question.

"Not from the footage we got, but we're looking further out. We'll find these fucking cunts. No fucker touches my brother and gets away with it. Plus—and you will flip your shit when I tell you this, man—his boyfriend, Harry," he snarls, and I nod. "He bolted. He didn't help him at all, just ran like a pussy,"

That little fucking cunt. I will add him to my hunt list. He will never see Ben again. No way in hell.

Mayhem and Ben have a wicked tight brotherhood. They are thick as thieves but as polar opposite as they come. There isn't anything these two men wouldn't do for each other and the ones they love. Like Ben and Logan. Those two are amazing to watch together: the way Ben teaches Logan things

Mayhem doesn't know; their love of dogs—that's what connects them more than anything.

Ben has a huge Saarloos Wolfdog called Friday. She is his shadow. Logan has a Bulldog called Winston. Even the two dogs are thick as thieves.

Again, silence fills the room. The thought of him being outnumbered makes my blood boil. I'm dying to seek revenge.

I click my knuckles, needing to do something with them. The need to rush out and find these fucks and make them pay for what they did to Ben is building, and I know I will blow my top sooner rather than later.

"I need to know what you're thinking, brother."

"Friday?" I blurt out, looking up at my brother.

He frowns at me. "What?"

"He'll want to see Friday when he wakes up. Send someone to get her. She'll keep him calm."

Shaking his head at me, he pinches the bridge of his nose.

"That is not what I meant and you motherfucking know it." His hands go to his hips, and he gives me a challenging look, daring me to not say what he wants me to say. From the way he's acting right now, it's clear he wants me to make my play for Ben, to come clean and claim him.

My feelings for Ben have always been bubbling under the surface but seeing his strength with fighting those fucks off has made them intensify. But I know that isn't what anyone needs right now.

Fuck me with a tailpipe.

"He just got the shit beat out of him, brother. His boyfriend ran off and left him. Give him some time. Let me talk to him first, but between us, yeah? I am claiming Ben as mine."

"About time, man." He slaps me on the back and steps over to the bed, leaning down to kiss his brother's head. "I'll get Friday here for him," he says as he walks over to the door.

"Get the prospect to bring me some food and drinks, will ya?" He nods.

"Yeah." With one last look at Ben, he leaves.

My gaze slides over Ben's prone body. The blood has been cleaned up and the cuts on his face patched up. The bruises are marring his handsome face, but fuck me, he still looks good.

Ben was cute when he was younger, but he grew better with age, like a fine, smooth whisky. He looks ten times fucking sexier when he has his facial hair. I think he heard me say that a time or two over the years, because it became a permanent feature on him.

He whimpers, gaining my attention. I move closer, kneeling on the floor next to the bed, the wood hard on my knees. My hand goes to his head, and I run my thick fingers through his short hair. He breathes in deeply, before his body settles down. I like knowing that it's my touch that is calming him, helping him settle back down

"Shh, baby. You're safe, Ben. Can you hear me?" I chance it and ask him.

He nods but doesn't open his eyes. Sweat covers his body. The doc said it would happen as his body is healing while he sleeps. His skin glistens with the little light that is coming from my bedside lamp.

My mouth waters at the sight. Sick, I know, but the way my body is responding to him while he is unconscious is telling me that it will be fucking epic when he is well and willing to take my cock.

My dick twitches in my jeans again as a quiet moan escapes his mouth. I reach over for the cloth and wet it again, then swipe it across his forehead and over his face. He winces in his sleep but doesn't wake.

Most of the brothers would laugh at me for acting like this because I am the worst fucking slut of the club. I don't bother with names, or even chit chat. When I want to fuck or get my dick sucked, I pick someone and get down to it.

The thing I love about being gay is that I don't have to deal with all the mushy feelings of getting a chick off and her thinking she is in love with me. The men I fuck are like me: they want to get off and are happy with that. Plus, I would break any bitch I fucked because I like to fuck hard and nasty. I can only fucking hope Ben likes that shit too.

"Leo." My name is a whisper on his lips, and my cock likes the sound of the breathy tone.

Fuck me, I sound like a chick swooning, as Lizzie calls it.

Ben's face scrunches up like he is in pain. His head rolls from side to side, and he calls out, "Scott"—Mayhem's real name. Then he calls my name again.

"I'm here. You're safe, babe. Breathe, relax."

With my hand on the top of his head, my thumb stroking back and forth, he settles down.

I smile, knowing it's me doing this shit. Not the drugs the doc gave him or his family, but me, my touch.

Over the years, I never thought I would want to settle down. Knowing that I enjoyed fucking random men, I stuck with it. It suited me. Then one day, Ben walked into the club looking like every gay man's wet dream.

I hadn't seen him in two years because he went travelling with friends. He left a boy and came back a man, with his short, scruffy beard and a new hair style, making him look even hotter.

Then, over the days, he got a haircut and shaved clean, which made him look his age again, so I dropped the comment that the facial hair suited him. After that, he grew it back and kept it tight and trim. He is one sexy bastard; I can tell you now.

Knowing that I couldn't have Ben because he was young and needed to live his life, I kept my feelings for him hidden and fucked everything that moved. I hurt him at one point, and I know that because he didn't come around for a few months after he caught me getting my dick sucked while I held eye contact with him and called out his name as I came.

I saw the pain but also the disgust in his eyes, and that cut me. The next time I saw him, he was with Harry—the prick, the pussy-arse fucking cunt I will gut the next time I see him. I will string him up with the fuckers who beat Ben. I will gut them all and watch as their blood flows. Then I will feed them to the pigs on a farm that a friend of mine owns.

Climbing to my feet, I move around the bed, pick up the chair, and move it closer so I can be on hand to touch Ben when he needs it. With my hand on the bed, I kick my feet up along the side of him and get some shut eye.

Tomorrow will bring new light, a fresh start, or some shit like that. All I see is another day to fucking bury myself in grease and drugs.

Life of a biker, aye.

Five

Ben

Blinking, I force my eyes open. As my eyes adjust to the light breaking through the blinds on the window, a few things hit me at once: I don't have blinds in my bedroom; the bed doesn't feel like mine; and I'm pretty sure my ceiling is a light grey, not white with cracks.

"You're at the clubhouse, in my room," comes a deep, gravelly voice from the side of the bed.

Turning my head, trying to ignore the sudden dizziness it causes, I see a tired looking Riot. He's dressed in only a pair of jeans, his muscled chest on full display for me to ogle. His long legs are resting on the bed, and he's barefoot. Can a man's feet be sexy? Because bloody hell, Riot's are.

I let out a sigh, happy I made it here. Thank fuck the men who helped me didn't take me to the hospital, because I knew the club would handle it, while the police would sit on their arses as it's only a gay man who was attacked.

"How long have I been out?" I ask, my throat dry. I cough, and Riot jumps up and fetches a bottle of water. He helps me sit up, and I wince against the pain that radiates through my ribs.

"Shit, that hurt."

"You need to take it easy. You had the shit beaten out of you, for fuck's sake," he reprimands.

"Thanks for the reminder." I scoff and Riot frowns at me, clearly not happy with my comeback.

"Don't get snarky with me, boy. They could have killed you." I look down at the blanket covering me from the waist down and get a glimpse of my torso.

No fucking wonder I'm in so much pain. From my chest to my hips, I'm pretty much black and blue.

"Well, they didn't—thanks to the guys who jumped in to help." I look up at him and find him giving me a dark look. I can't determine if it's because he's pissed at me for mouthing off, pissed at the guys who beat me, or pissed because I'm half naked in his bed.

He shakes his head and stands up, before pacing back and forth in front of the bed. His hands come up to grip the back of his neck, fingers lacing together, as if he's trying to restrain himself from tearing out of here, finding the men who beat me, and sending them to meet their maker.

Riot has always been the guy who will make you laugh when you are down, who makes light of a situation, but bloody hell can he be a mean son of a bitch when the situation calls for it.

After years of watching him, I know he feels things deeply and is willing to die and kill to protect the ones he loves: the men in the club and their families. And despite that readiness to commit violence, he will be the first one to get on the floor with the kids and play with their toys and walk the dog when needed. He freaking loves dogs, mine included.

Speaking of dogs…

"Friday—I need to go home for her," I tell him and try to move from the bed. My body screams at me to stay put, to rest up, but my baby is home alone, and she doesn't like being alone for extended periods of time.

Riot stops pacing and rushes to my side, still looking pissed at me.

"Boy, you really need to learn when your body is telling you to stop this stupid shit. You are hurt and need rest. Friday is on her way here. Mayhem has sent a prospect to go and fetch her. They should be here soon."

I sigh and let him help me sit back on the bed. With my eyes closed, I try to breathe through the pain every movement causes. Riot growls under his breath. I open my eyes to see him walking over to the small desk he has in his room. He picks up a pack of painkillers before handing them to me, along with the bottle of water I dropped when I stood up.

"You need to stay on top of the pain, boy," he huffs, and I nod.

"Can you do me a favour, Riot?" I ask him. He looks at me waiting for me to continue. "Can you please, for the love of God, stop fucking calling me 'boy'? I'm twenty-seven for crying out loud. I am not some kid," I snap, and he smirks at me before he throws his head back and laughs.

"Prick," I mutter. His laughter stops, and then he's on the bed in a flash, his hip flush with my thigh.

My breath hitches in my throat at the sudden contact. We haven't been this close before and it takes me a second to control my body's reaction to him. My nipples pebble, and I know he can see them because his gaze drops before coming back up to meet mine.

My dick is straining in the boxers I'm wearing. They must have stripped me when I got here. Fuck, did Riot or the doc remove my clothes?

"Who undressed me?" The question escapes me before I can stop it.

He leans in so close I can feel his breath on my face, and my body perks up. Riot licks his lips, before dropping his gaze to my mouth, then looking back up at me.

36

"I did—with the help of the doc. We needed to see the extent of your injuries. And to answer your previous question, I know you're not a boy, believe me. Do I look like the kind of man who fantasises about fucking a boy into my mattress?" I shake my head because I seem to have lost the ability to speak.

He smirks and gently grips my throat, making my eyes widen with arousal and shock. But not fear. Never fear. I know Riot would never hurt me.

"Good. For years I've waited to have you in this bed, but not like this. So fair warning, Ben, I—"

The door swings open, stopping him from finishing his sentence. We both look over to see my brother standing there, looking between Riot and me. His face shows no emotion, so I'm not sure if he will flip his shit at how close we are or not.

"Did I interrupt something, brothers?" I go to speak but Riot gets there first.

"Yeah, you did," he growls. I bring my gaze back to him, seeing him scowling at my brother, who then smirks.

A clicking on the hardwood floor in the hallway sounds, stealing my attention. Riot's gaze drops, and his face softens.

"Friday, come." Like the obedient dog she is, she listens to Riot and leaps up onto the bed, then commando crawls to me. Sensing I'm hurt, she whines as she gets closer.

"Come here, baby," I call to her.

She rests her head on my lower stomach, trying to get as close to me as possible. My fingers delve into her soft fur, and the feel of her being close to me calms down my rapidly beating heart. One thing Friday does is calm me down. She helps with my anxiety, and she knows when I need her.

"Good girl." Riot soothes her too, rewarding her for her gentleness.

"Thanks for bringing her." I look to my brother, who smiles at me.

37

"It was Riot's idea. He said you'd want her here, so I sent a prospect over to your place to get her. Also, Lizzie went with and packed you some clothes. She is chomping at the bit to get in here and see you. I can hold her off for a little longer, but no can do with Logan, Benny Boy. Sorry, kid." He smirks.

"I'm not sure Logan should see me like this, Scott. It looks like I went ten rounds with Hulk, and then Thor finished me off." I laugh.

Yep, I am a huge Marvel nerd, hence my dog's name.

"Fair enough. Brother, we have church. We need to go over the information we found." Scott drags his gaze from mine and looks at Riot, who nods at his instruction. "I'll leave you to it then. I'll keep Logan at bay for now, Benny, but he will want to see you soon." With a nod from me, he leaves.

The room is quiet, and I hate it because I want to ask Riot what he was going to say before my brother came in and interrupted but I'm not sure I have the guts to ask.

We both run our fingers through Friday's fur, and I keep my attention on her while I try to build my courage. When I finally raise my gaze and look at Riot, I find him watching me intently. He doesn't say anything right away. He just sits there looking at me, and it starts to give me a complex.

My stomach grumbles, breaking the silence between us, and he smiles. Friday cocks her head with a little questioning sound. I laugh and look back to Riot. The smile on his face is freaking handsome, and it makes my stomach clench.

"How about I go and get you something to eat? Maybe something for this little miss too." He ruffles Friday's fur.

"She only eats raw food, Riot, unless you have some dog snacks for her," I explain.

"I have some peanut butter buttons here. I know she loves them." Fuck me, my heart swoons over his observation of what my dog loves.

I tried hard not to feel these things for Riot, because I know he isn't one to settle for being with one man, but when he does shit like this, it makes it ten times harder for me to resist.

"Thanks."

Before he gets off the bed, he closes the distance between our faces again, and I suck in a deep breath, holding it while waiting to see what he does next.

I'm not a virgin—far from it—but bloody hell, this man makes me feel like a teenage boy when he's near me. My gaze drops to his lips, which are surrounded by stubble that he keeps at a fashionable length, like me. Lips I want to feel pressed against mine and wrapped around my cock.

His scent and the sexual vibes that are coming from him has my body buzzing and momentarily forgetting the pain.

"We'll finish this conversation soon, babe. Too much time has been wasted, and I am not wasting another motherfucking second of it." Leaning in, he kisses the corner of my mouth, before moving away. He picks up a t-shirt and his cut, then leaves the room before I can so much as register what he just did.

What the hell?

Riot just kissed me, albeit on the corner of my mouth. He has never done anything like that before. What does it mean? Fuck!

Friday moves with me as I gently shift down the bed, and we snuggle as best I can in a position that doesn't cause me more pain before I slip into a dreamless sleep.

Six

Riot

Chaos sits at the head of the table in the room we call Church, gavel in hand, ready to start the meeting, as we all take our seats. We're discussing the shit that went down with Ben two days ago. He has been here since, healing up, being pampered by the women.

In that time, we were able to get some info on the fucks who beat him, but we can't fucking find them. They're part of a punk-arse gang that roams the streets at night, causing trouble. They look for fights and drama and are the type to stir the pot. It's because of them and their crew that a peaceful protest turned violent just a few months ago.

"They started on the cops and the cops fought back. Don't get me wrong, I hate pigs, but if they don't deserve shit then they don't deserve it. A female officer was brutally beaten by the little shits. Three guys beat up one chick. It's not right, man," Keys states to the room.

I nod, my anger towards these fucks building. They hurt my man. Fuck me, that sounds both strange and good at the same time.

"I want first dibs on these motherfuckers," I snarl, my fists clenched tight on my thighs.

40

Mayhem looks at me from across the table. He cocks an eyebrow at me, but I don't say shit to him.

He knows how I feel about Ben, but I kept myself on a tight leash when it came to him out of respect to my club brother. We are protective to a fault, and loyal, and I wouldn't do anything to jeopardise the relationship we have. Plus, I would never come between blood brothers.

With each passing year, I had to watch as Ben grew into a man. A man who got better and better with age. Not only in looks but in brains. He has done amazing for himself, and I am proud as fuck of him.

Seeing him with the very few boyfriends he's had made me pissed off that he wasn't with me. So, I did what every man would do: I buried myself in the arses of random men. Whenever Mayhem talked about Ben hooking up with someone, I went off the fucking rails. I fucked so many random men and drank so much I often blacked the hell out.

My drinking got so bad that I woke up one morning and found a chick in bed with me. To this day I have no idea what the fuck happened. She said we fucked, but I have no recollection.

From that day on, I reeled my drinking in, only having a few beers and one or two whiskies, which is my drink of choice. A whisky and a cigar is my perfect night. Fuck what people think. I may look like a dirty biker and act like one from time to time, but I enjoy the finer things in life.

Ben is one of those finer things. I just need to tell him and Mayhem that this needs to happen. Like I told Ben, way too much fucking time has been wasted between us, but no more.

I respect the fuck out of my brothers, but I also have to respect myself and my heart.

"Riot, are you with us or the motherfucking fairies?" I hear Chaos call to me.

41

"The fairies. They're more interesting than you motherfuckers," I joke. The guys chuckle, but Chaos looks like he wants to rip my head off.

"We need to track the pricks down and make them pay for laying a hand on my brother. I know Ben would have handled himself if it was one on one, but fuck me, three on one… that shit is cheap and weak," Mayhem snaps.

I feel what he is saying because I want to kill the fuckers for hurting Ben, and yeah, he could have taken one on in a fair fight, but these scumbags don't fight fair.

"I want in." I lock eyes with Mayhem. Neither of us say anything for fuck knows how long. I let him know without words that I will protect Ben—protect what is mine. He gives me a nod, and his mouth quirks to the side.

That may be the only sign of a blessing I get from him right now and fuck me I will take it.

Years ago, when I decided to keep my distance from him, I was letting him grow, find his feet so to speak, but it was also out of respect for Mayhem and the club. They all see Ben as a baby brother. I was the only one who didn't have brotherly thoughts when thinking of him, but like a brother I would protect him with my life.

I'm getting up there in years now, and it's time to settle the fuck down. Witnessing my brothers find their old ladies has made me want what they have. I want an old man. A man who I know can handle club life; the way we rule things, and the way shit goes down in our lives.

I need Ben Miller.

But I know I need to tread carefully with him. He just got the crap beaten out of him and his boyfriend bolted, not helping him, or even calling for help. The prick just ran like the pussy he is.

"Has anyone tried finding the prick boyfriend?" I call out to the table.

"Nope. The cunt ran. He doesn't deserve to know how my brother is," Mayhem snaps, and murmurs of agreement go around the table.

"Can't believe he ran and left Ben. That is some fucked up shit right there," one of my brother's pipes in, and I nod.

Watching the hard men around the room accepting Ben as one of their own, even though he doesn't wear a patch, makes me love my club even more. They don't give a fuck that he's gay, nor that I am.

You would think that a bunch of dirty, horny bikers wouldn't want to watch another man get his dick sucked by another man, but they don't shy away from it. Sex is sex in this club. Like the world says, *love is love*.

My fingers flex as I think of Ben on his knees, sucking my cock, his soft lips surrounding my shaft as I slide in and out of his wet mouth; his stubble catching the sensitive skin, making my balls crave release.

Licking my lips, I look down at my hard dick pressing against the rough denim of my jeans. My heart rate picks up at just picturing Ben before me, so fuck knows how I'll feel when he has his hands on me. Just the thought has pre-cum leaking from the slit in my cock.

Something hard hits my face, and I look up at the table and see a coaster. Frowning, I pick the offending item up and look around the table at my brothers, seeing them all smirking, but Mayhem is scowling at me.

"What the fuck, brother?"

"I may be okay with you wanting my brother, but fuck me, I do not want to see you have a daydream about fucking him. Damn, fucker, that is just straight up wrong," he gripes, and it makes me laugh.

"Hey, it's payback for all the times I've had to listen to you and Lizzie fuck."

The boys laugh, until Chaos opens his mouth, bringing the serious shit back to the table.

"Shut the fuck up. Keys, carry on getting more information on this so-called crew. We need to make a plan to take them down. I think the world would be a better place without them," he states, and I nod in agreement.

Keys gives Prez a chin lift, and he ends Church.

As I leave the room, I feel the heat of Mayhem's stare. Looking at him over my shoulder, I stop and turn around when I see the scowl on his face.

"What?"

"Are you serious about Ben or is this just a chance to fuck him out of your system?" he asks me. Shaking my head at him, I step closer, noticing all the chatter in the room has stopped.

"Are you really asking me that after all the motherfucking years I held off because of you?"

My voice drops to a deep tone, showing my anger towards my brother. He knows how I feel about Ben, so I have no fucking clue why he is asking me this stupid question.

Most of the club know how I feel, but they also know my respect for Mayhem and his family runs deep with me. There is no way I would fuck it out with Ben just to get him out of my system. I have more respect for the man than his blood brother is giving me credit for right now.

Mayhem shrugs, his gaze still locked on mine. My lips thin, and my nostrils flare with anger. My fists clench, but before I can blow a fucking gasket, I hear my name being called.

"Riot, Ben is asking for you." Looking to my left, I see Evie, Psycho's old lady.

I send her a smile and a nod, then give Mayhem one more look before marching off to my room to see what Ben wants. Shaking my head to clear my pissed off mood, I reach my door and push it open.

As girly as it sounds, my breath gets caught in my fucking lungs when I see Ben sitting up in my bed, his bare chest on full display.

Fuck me, waiting has never been so fucking hard, and hard is one thing I am.

Seven

Ben

Sitting in the main room at the clubhouse, I watch the half-naked women prance around, thinking they are sexy, but all I see is desperation. Hell, I can bloody smell it.

It's been a few days since I had the shit beaten out of me. My whole torso is still sore to touch, so showering is a bitch, and my face is still bruised to hell, though some of the swelling is going down. I can't shave and my short beard is growing out, so I'm starting to look like a freaking mountain man.

"You, okay?" Lizzie's voice comes from my left. Looking at her, I give her a smile and nod.

"Yeah. Just wondering how you and the other women cope with all this rubbish floating around." I nod to one of the girls, who is hanging desperately over one of the single brothers.

I know they try it on with the married ones. They come around to hook up with a biker, taken or not. Some men in MC's do cheat, and some say it's okay because they're bikers and it's expected. Hell, I've seen TV shows and there is cheating in that, but I don't tolerate cheating.

46

I've been cheated on before and it sucks. Being in an MC does not give you a free pass to fuck anyone you want when you have a partner at home waiting for you.

If you want to fuck someone else, then break off the relationship you're in. It's that simple. Do not be a greedy twat and try to have both. People only get hurt in the end. It isn't worth the pain.

"It's hard sometimes, but I trust Scott. I know he wouldn't cheat on me. There's too much at stake for him." She winks at me, and I smile.

She is perfect for my brother. She knows how to handle him, and she loves Logan like he is her own blood.

"He loves you," I state truthfully.

"He does. What about you? Have you heard from Harry?" she asks me, then sips her tea.

"Nope. Nothing. I refuse to send him a text. If he wanted to check on me, he could have called or text, but he hasn't, so…" I shrug.

Thinking about not hearing from my so-called boyfriend, I think I dodged a future bullet with him. "We're done. I can't be a with a man who likes to play games like he has in the past. And how can I be with someone who genuinely doesn't give a flying fuck about me, after he saw three guys beat me up?"

I shrug. Surely, I should feel upset that my relationship with Harry is finally over, but if anything, I feel relief. The last year has been a struggle with him. It seemed like I was the only one putting anything into our relationship.

My gaze moves from my sister-in-law to scan the room. I spot my brother sitting in the corner with some of his brothers, Riot included. I let my gaze glide over his body, taking in his short, dark hair that's shaved on the sides and longer on top, and the way his white t-shirt pulls against his biceps.

47

He has a foot resting on the coffee table in front of him, the position making his jeans tighten around his powerful thighs, showing off the shapely muscles I would love to see bare—while I'm up close and personal with them, with his dick in my mouth.

I clear my throat and adjust the way I'm sitting to try and hide the sudden tenting of my jogging bottoms. Not a good thing to happen with the kids running around and while sitting next to Lizzie.

As if he can sense me looking at him, Riot turns his head, his gaze connecting with mine. His lips quirk at the corner, then he winks at me, and my dick goes rock solid in seconds.

My heart is pounding. This is what this man does to me. I'm not usually one to be shy around men, but Riot, aka Leo Peters, has me acting like a fucking teenage boy.

When I bite my lip, I see his eyes darken. Even from across the room, I swear on my life I hear him growl, and if my brother's reaction is anything to go by, I can safely say he did.

We stay locked in a heated stare, until someone walks between us, forcing the break. I blink, and the person who cuts us off comes into view. It's some guy I've seen around the club a few times. He leans in so close to Riot I think he's about to kiss him.

If he kisses him, I'm going to be sick.

My stomach churns and my lungs scream for oxygen as I hold my breath, waiting to see what will happen. I feel Lizzie grab my hand, but I don't look at her. I physically *can't* pull my eyes away from Riot and the man who has now dropped to his haunches to get to eye level with him.

I watch in slow motion as Riot smiles at the man, who returns the smile before touching him, making Riot's smile widen. Is this what it's like to be with a biker? To sit and watch as men fawn over them? That is something I one hundred percent refuse to do.

Like I've said, I do not play games. No fucking way.

They talk for a little while longer, and I can't take it. Slowly pushing to my feet with one hand on the arm of the sofa and the other holding my ribs, I wince in pain, but I push it down and leave the room, not looking in the men's direction. I just want out of this room so I can pack up my shit and leave.

"Friday," I call to my baby, and she follows.

As straight as I can walk, I make my way into the room I have been staying in, which incidentally is Riot's room. I let Friday in, and she jumps onto the bed, walks in a circle, then settles.

Scanning the room, I spot my kit bag and some of my clothes. While holding my ribs tightly, I bend down and pick my things up, then throw them in the bag. I hear Friday whine, and I glance over to her, only to see her staring at the door. Looking over my shoulder, I see Riot leaning against the doorframe, scowling at me.

"Going somewhere?" His voice is deep, firm, and it does silly shit to my body.

This man belongs on the end of a sex phoneline. I bet men and women would come running to get off from listening to him telling them what to do.

Looking back to my bag, I wince at the sudden twinge in my ribs but push the pain down. I need to go home and finish up my book, which I have lost two fucking days on.

I hear him shuffle closer, but I don't look at him. I keep packing—albeit slowly, but I do it anyway.

"I'm leaving," I state, trying to keep the pain out of my voice.

"Yeah, I don't think so. You still need to heal. Plus, the fuckers are still out there," he spits out.

Turning on my heel to face the broody bastard, I close my eyes as a wave of pain hits me, and suddenly feel sick to my stomach. I feel heat just before a hand cups my jaw, making my eyes spring open. Riot is so close. His chest is brushing against mine, and my dick likes the feel of him being nearby.

Shit, not now.

"First of all, the guys who beat me up didn't target me on purpose. I was in the wrong place at the wrong time. They didn't track me, so they don't know where I live. Secondly, you are not my brother, nor my boyfriend, so you don't get a say in that capacity either." I huff, pulling some much-needed air into my lungs.

Ranting with possible fractured ribs and a bruised torso is not a good idea. I watch as Riot's scowl deepens, his eyes dark as he steps closer to me. Licking my lips, I draw his gaze down to my mouth, before he licks his own and looks back up to meet my gaze.

"They may not have targeted you, but you never fucking know with cunts like them. We've done some recon and found out they like to cause shit, so I wouldn't be surprised if they did seek you out, especially knowing how important you are to the club."

I straighten my shoulders and steel my spine, ignoring the ache in my abdomen.

"Just the club?" slips out before I can stop the stupid fucking words. Fucking hell. Why me?

I turn back to my bag, and just as I add in my charger, a hand grips mine, stopping any more movement. To say my body goes into overdrive at his touch would be a complete understatement.

I close my eyes and wait for his words, even though I'm betting on him saying no, that he cares but that's all he can give. There have been so many mixed signals from Riot over the years that sometimes I don't know if I'm coming or going.

Just when I think we are in a good place, that he might ask me out, he pulls back and fucks some random bloke. That's why I stayed away from the club. I can't cope with the whiplash he gives me.

"Not just the club." His chest is plastered to my back, his breath caressing my neck, making goosebumps break out over my skin as my nipples pebble. The thin t-shirt I'm wearing does not do a good job of hiding that fact.

I clear my throat and try to turn, but he's standing so close to me, caging me in. His musky scent invades my senses, and a groan slips out. He has always smelled good, like oil and sandalwood.

He presses closer, until I can feel his erection against my arse cheek.

"Stay. I need to know you're safe." His voice is firm, leaving no room for argument. Then he drops it deeper. "Plus, I like you in my bed."

I close my eyes and take in the sound, letting it wash over me as his hands find my hips and he presses even closer.

"Fuck," I mutter, making him chuckle.

"I need you close. I'll take you home in a few days; once I know it's clear or we find the little shits."

"I'm not the only one you want close," I state.

Sliding out from his hold, I release the breath I was holding. Being around him, this close, has my body reacting in way that's hazardous to me.

Bringing my head up, our gazes connect again, and I find Riot grinning at me, giving a perfect view of his white teeth that are framed by sexy lips and stubble that makes him look like a biker god.

"Jealous, Benny?" I frown at him; at the way he asks in a joking manner.

"Don't call me that. Why would I be jealous? I don't own you. You can shag whoever the hell you want," I snap and pick my bag up.

Childish, maybe, but I don't give a fuck. I am too fucking old to play games with a man who likes to fuck around. All I

51

want is to find a man who will adore and love me; support and respect me, as much as I would him.

Every relationship is a two-way street. It's all about give and take.

When I step around him and over to the door, his arms shoot out, stopping me from leaving. I growl in frustration, making his eyes darken with lust. Shit.

"I said I want you to stay. And going by the way your body reacted to me, you want to stay too."

"And clearly you have others who are more than happy to keep your bed warm for you. I'm going home, Riot." I push his arm away, and I'm so caught up in the stare off between us that I forget about my ribs.

I growl out in pain, almost blacking out from it. Riot picks me up and lies me on the bed, resting his hands on either side of me, stopping me from moving. His face moves closer, his gaze locked on mine, and he licks his lips.

"No one else has been in this bed, *ever*. When I've fucked, it has been at their place or out in the open." I wince at the reminder that he's fucked so many people. "I'm no fucking saint, babe. You know that. You have known me for fucking years, and the shit I've done. You can't hold that against me.

"I also know you want me just as much as I want you, but you've just got the shit beaten out of you and your fucking cunt of a boyfriend ran like a pussy, so I know you have to deal with that shit. I will have you, Ben, and only you."

"So, who the hell was that bloke out there? I'm not playing games, Riot. You want to shag other men, do it, but leave me the fuck out of it. Yeah, I need to deal with this," I wave my hand down my body, "and Harry, but fuck me, I'm an adult who knows what he wants. It's you who can't make up his mind. I'm sick of the mixed signals from you. We are way too bloody old to be acting like this."

"That was a guy I hooked up with weeks ago. He wanted more, and I told him to fuck off," he tells me, and I scoff.

"Yeah, you really told him to 'fuck off,'" I reply sarcastically, using air quotes. "That was clear with all the touching and smiling. Good job there, bud," I rant, and with each passing word, his smile grows bigger and bigger, fuelling my anger.

"Laugh all you want, *Leo*. I'm not doing this," I say, using his birth name, something not many people do.

We stay there in silence, time ticking away, neither of us saying anything. My heart is beating like there's a pack of alpacas dancing on my chest, as this man sorts through what I just told him. Every second that passes, I think he's going to leave; just say, 'Fuck it, you're too much hard work'. In reality, I am so freaking low maintenance it drives my friends crazy.

I don't need all the pretty frills to enjoy my life. Family, friends, food, and drinks, and not forgetting my books, is me in a nutshell.

All the glitz and glamour, drinking every weekend, going to parties and shows, is not me. A night in with a beer is more my speed.

His eyes narrow, and I hold my breath as I watch him adjust his cut, then step over to the door. Fuck. He looks over his shoulder with one hand on the door handle.

I track the way his bicep and shoulder bunch as he clutches the handle, his strong jaw set tight as he looks at me, with a look that has my heart skipping a beat.

"Stay put," is all he says.

I growl in frustration again as he pulls the door open, walks out, and closes it behind him without a backward glance.

What the hell was that?

"Fucking broody bikers," I mutter. Friday curls up to my side and I snuggle her as I fall into a much-needed sleep.

Who knew getting the shit kicked out of you could leave you so drained and tired all the time? It's something to add to my mental note bank for a future book, well that plus how truly broody bikers can be.

Eight

Riot

Slamming my hammer against the door panel, I nod in satisfaction when the panel fits in perfectly, hiding the shit-tonne of drugs hidden behind it. I added some into the space beneath the back seat, and in the roof.

It's all about the balance and placement. Not only do I stock up cars, but I do boats and larger vehicles. Besides the custom garage that me and Mayhem mostly work in, the club does a lot of other shit, like collect money owed to the club. We also have a bar called Wreckers and a tattoo shop called Twisted Skin.

"How's that look, brother?" Chaos calls out to me as he walks into the garage.

Getting to my feet, I toss the hammer onto the workbench with a loud clatter, but I don't give a fuck. I've been in a pissy mood all day because Ben is going home tomorrow, and I don't have a fucking excuse to keep him here. Picking up a cloth, I clean off my hands. The dust and shit from the material behind the door panel clings to them, making them itch.

"All done. I need to try and fix that bulge in the Ranger Rover, but it shouldn't give me too much shit," I explain and step over to the fridge, pulling it open and picking up a beer. I offer one to Prez, and he takes it.

"Good. We need to make that shipment. The buyers are getting antsy about needing more product. Fuckers are selling it quicker than we can supply it, and if we don't keep up with the demand, they'll look to someone else to buy from," he tells me, and I nod.

"They wouldn't dare piss on our deal, mate. We will get them their supply. We just need to up the numbers on our side." He grunts his agreement.

"Hey, fuckers," Mayhem calls as he comes to a stop next to Prez.

"Prick," I mutter.

Mayhem smirks and sits on the stool next to the car. Since he said that shit to me the other day, he's been looking at me differently, like he finally sees I'm serious about claiming Ben when the time is right for the man. Don't get me wrong, I am a fucking cunt when I want to be, but if I want things to work out with Ben and not die a lonely old man, then I need to do this the right way.

"You still moping around?" They chuckle at Mayhem's question.

"Fuck off," I snap, flipping the fucker off.

Turning my back to them, I get on with my work, bending some thin metal bars to hold the drugs in place, making sure they're not bulking so they stick out or stop the panels from reattaching.

The work today was supposed to keep my mind off Ben, who is still sleeping in my bed. Him and the fucking dog. For the past week I've been sleeping in a spare room at the club, or some nights I've fallen sleep in the chair in my room, watching as Ben sleeps, touching him when he has a nightmare. He knows I've been there, but not once has he asked me to get into the bed with him. Maybe I should have just done it, not giving a fuck what he says.

"Question for you, Riot," Mayhem speaks again.

"What now, fuckface?" I growl and turn to face the prick.

"Are you pissed because Ben is leaving, or because you haven't had your cock sucked in a week?" He winks, and I throw the first thing I lay my hands on at him, which happens to be the hammer I was using.

He dodges the thing, laughing his arse off. Prez joins in with the laughing, but I know I can't do fuck all to him. I value my fucking life.

"Fuck you." I sigh and sit down on the box we keep as a seat. The two men look at me, waiting for an explanation.

"Not my type, brother. Now give me a set of juicy tits and a nice, round arse and I am there." Mayhem wiggles his eyebrows.

"Don't let Lizzie hear you calling her a nice set of tits and arse," Chaos tells him with a smug look on his face.

Blowing out a breath, I look Mayhem in the eyes and give it to him straight. No time for fucking around anymore.

"Listen, he's been through some shit, what with the beating and the pussy punk-ass bitch," I spit out. "I respect the fuck out of you, brother. That's why I've kept my distance from him over the years. I wasn't right for him—fuck, I don't think I ever will be—but seeing him beat up the way he was triggered something in me. The need to kill everyone who put their hands on him, to feel their life drain away, makes my dick hard."

"Not sure how I feel about your dick getting hard over spilling blood, but each to their own, I guess," Mayhem jokes.

Chuckling, I carry on. "It will happen; I can tell you that now, brother. So be fucking warned. No more time wasting. I'm making a move—albeit a slow one, but he will know the end game." I take a deep breath, then chug from my beer.

"Maybe just claim him. Fuck all the rest. He knows the way of the club, and he will make a good old man, but you need to stop fucking other people if he's what you want," Prez adds.

"I don't get why you're still waiting around. Fucking claim him already. We all know how you feel about him, and him you. Hell, we all see the fuck-me eyes you give each other."

"I told you all of this," I spit out, but Mayhem just shakes his head.

"Fucking excuses, if you ask me, man. I don't think you're serious at all about my brother, so you need to nut up or shut up. Make a move on my brother or keep fucking random arseholes who have no name or face. Spend the rest of your life watching my brother find a man who will keep him and not flake the fuck out, like you are." He's pissed. His eyes are narrowed on me, and his nostrils are flaring. Fuck.

Shaking my head at him, I look him in the eye, not happy with the shit he's throwing at me.

"Who I'm fucking has nothing to do with you or anyone. Where I stick my dick is not up for discussion. I'm a thirty-six-year-old man, for fuck's sake. I've been fucking since I was fourteen, and I will keep fucking until the day I die. No one tells me what the hell to do, brother. Bollocks to that."

Someone clears their throat, making my stomach tighten, because I know who it is before I even turn my head to look. I catch the look on Mayhem's face, and he's clearly not happy.

"Hey, Benny boy. What's up?" he calls out to Ben. Fuck my life with a hot exhaust pipe.

"The sky," he answers, earning chuckles from his brother and Chaos.

That little answer is something Logan and Ben started when they saw each other, and it's stuck with others in the club too.

Sometimes the answers get a little, or a lot, dirty and sexual.

Twisting in my seat, I gaze up at Ben, who is looking fucking hot today in a green t-shirt and a pair of light blue jeans that have scuffs and holes in them. His scruff is a little longer, which I know he hates. He likes trimmed facial hair.

"I was coming out to see if you could give me a ride home. I think Friday is missing her bed, and to be honest, so am I," he states, not bothering to look at me.

I don't have to ask how much of my rant he heard, because the way he's avoiding my eyes makes me think he heard pretty much all of it. Hearing him say that he wants out of my bed is like a punch to the gut.

We have talked over the last few days, when I haven't been doing shit for the club, and he's been tapping away on his laptop, not working but doing the social media side to his business. He needs to mingle with other authors, apparently, so they help share his book, and he does the same with their books.

Tit for tat. I can respect that.

He hasn't mentioned going back to his house once in the times we've talked. What the fuck? I'm pissed, and I need to know why the fuck he's running, because that is what he's doing. Fucking running.

Clearing my throat, I get to my feet and move toward him. He's all I see as I stop inches from him. He only needs to look up a fraction because he isn't much shorter than me.

"What's got you running?" He frowns at my question. He looks taken aback, if I'm being honest, but I don't give a fuck right now. He never told me he wanted to go home early.

"Nothing. I just want to go home. I'm moving around a lot better on my own. It's time."

"Oh, yeah? So why haven't you said anything to me?" I cross my arms over my chest, drawing his eyes down to my biceps, which I know he likes to look at. Every time we're in my room and I go shirtless, I catch him looking at my arms.

Okay, so I flex a little for his eyes only, but hey, I want the guy so peacocking it is.

His eyes harden, and I know he heard what I just said about my fucking activities. I smirk at him, and his lips thin in anger, but that only makes my dick hard.

"I don't have to tell you shit, Riot."

"Keep up the attitude, babe. It's making my cock hard." Someone coughs behind me, but I ignore them, keeping my gaze firmly locked on Ben.

We stand in a stare off, and I hear shuffling behind me, but again I keep my gaze trained on the man in front of me. The one man who can get my dick throbbing with a simple look, and I know I do that to him too.

The chemistry between us is fucking rocketing to the moon and back.

"Tell me why you want to go home early. We had plans to take you home in a day or two," I try again, but I can see he's going to be a stubborn little shit.

His mouth twists before he speaks. "Again, I don't need to tell you fuck all. I want to go home, and I will. Maybe you can have one of your many nameless or faceless fucks keep you company while I'm gone. I'm sure a man like you doesn't like going too long without sex, so I'll get out of your hair," he snaps, and looks around me to his brother. "Fuck," he mutters. It has me looking over my shoulder, and I grin.

Mayhem and Prez have left, no doubt letting us talk this shit out. They aren't ones for drama—not that we're causing it, but I am surprised to see Mayhem leaving his brother to me.

"Looks like you're stuck with me after all," I quip, but Ben doesn't find it funny.

"I told you a few days ago that I'm not playing games, Riot. Go and shag some unfortunate bloke because I am going home. I have a book to finish."

60

He spins on his heels and marches back toward the clubhouse.

"What did you really come out here for, babe?" I call out to him, which causes him to stop in his tracks.

He stares at me, a look on his face that I can't read, and I don't like that shit.

"It doesn't matter now," is his reply, and he goes to walk off again.

"*Ben.*" I growl out his name, and he stops and pivots on his feet, his face showing me stone features.

"What, Riot?" he snaps.

"*Everything* between me and you matters. Tell me," I demand.

Looking around, he tucks his hands in the front pocket of his jeans, careful of his ribs. The movement shows off the defined muscles of his biceps, and I can completely understand the meaning of arm porn now, which I've heard the old ladies talking about.

"I was going to ask if you wanted to take Friday for a walk with me, but I'm good with going on my own." With his final words, he turns and walks back into the building, leaving me to my own devices and thoughts.

Fuck. Why do I keep fucking up with my big mouth?

Cursing, I spin on my heel and run my hand through my short hair, before walking back into the garage to finish up my job for the day. I need to make sure all the parts are back in place and looking like they haven't been tampered with.

Nine

Ben

It's the day after my little spat with Riot and I haven't seen him. My brother told me he had some shit to do, so he left to deal with that. I'm pissed and disappointed that he didn't tell me he was leaving, but I know I have no claim over him, as I've told him. But it still sucks that he didn't tell me.

God my head is screwed.

I look around the room one more time, making sure I haven't missed anything, because I'm going home today. Friday is by the door, itching to get out of this room, and to be honest so am I. Smiling, I lift my bag up, wincing slightly at the dull pain in my ribs.

It's only been a few days, and my ribs feel better, but damn, they still hurt if I catch myself off guard. Friday whines when I hiss in pain, but I ruffle her fur.

"I'm okay, girl. Come on, let's go home." I pull the door open but stop my next steps.

Riot is leaning against the wall, his ankles and arms crossed. The leather jacket he's wearing looks like it's straining against his muscle. Bloody hell, he looks like a biker god, and it's simply not fucking fair.

His head comes up and he looks at me, then down to my bags. I know he isn't happy with me going home yet, but honestly, I couldn't care less. The need to sleep in my own bed is overwhelming, and the need to finish my book is itching at my skin.

Friday steps over to him, rubs against his legs and he leans down a little to scratch behind her ears.

"Is that everything?" he asks, nodding to my bags.

"Yeah. Come, Friday."

She steps close to me, and I go to walk past him, but he takes my bags from my hand. I go to tell him to bugger off, but the look in his eyes stops me from saying anything. He looks pissed. His eyes are darker than normal, and not in the sexy way.

His anger is showing, and it's a look that isn't usually directed at me. I mutter a "thanks", and I get a grunt for it.

Sighing, I follow him out to my brother's Ranger Rover. I watch as Riot places my bags and Friday's things into the boot, then he pulls open the back passenger door for her to jump inside while I say my goodbyes to my brother and the club.

"We are always here for you, Ben. You know that," Chaos calls to me, and I nod.

"Thanks for having me. I just hope I didn't put anyone out."

"You didn't put anyone out, and if they have shit to say, they can fucking say it to my face," Riot snaps from behind me.

I watch as the brothers of the club smirk at him, then give me chin lifts, then I get into the car. Looking behind me, I check on Friday, making sure she's strapped into her harness.

The drive to my house is quiet and awkward, but I bet that's only on my side because Riot doesn't do awkward. Oh no, this man does cocky, confident, and sexy all in one package. He has no reason to be awkward. We pull into my

63

short driveway, and I get out of the car to unhook Friday so she can run around my small front garden.

"She seems happy," comes his voice.

"Yeah. She is," I chuckle. I go to say something, but Riot swears, drawing my attention to him.

Turning around, I see Harry walking in front of my house and then down my driveway. He looks happy, smiling and all fake. Why the hell didn't I see this shit sooner?

"Baby," he calls to me as he gets closer. He leans in for a kiss, but I jerk back, making him frown. Riot growls and steps closer to me. "What?" Harry asks.

"Are you fucking shitting me right now?" I ask him with a snarl. He has the cheek to look shocked by my reaction.

"What? What is going on here, Ben?" Harry looks between Riot and me, his eyes going wide, and he takes a step back, again having the fucking audacity to look shocked and hurt. "Are you cheating on me? With him?" He waves his hand at Riot and me.

Riot snarls, stepping closer, but I place my hand on his chest, stopping him from beating Harry to a pulp, because he would do that in a heartbeat. I watch as Harry's eyes go wide with fear, but they also track me touching the biker next to me.

"No cheating. All I ever gave you was loyalty and respect. Can you say the same for me? I got the fuck beat out of me a few days ago and you bloody ran like a pussy. You never helped me or called the police. Not once have you tried to contact me in the days I've been recovering at the clubhouse. You call yourself a boyfriend when all you do is think of yourself. In a relationship, you look out for the people you love and care about. You did none of those things for me. You played games, and you know how much I fucking hate games. It's black and white in my world. Simple as fuck, no frills. If anyone ever cheated in this relationship, it was you, Harry. You always liked to see how other men would gush

64

over you. Well, I can I tell you right fucking now there will be no more gushing from me, you fucking arsehole," I fume at him.

Taking a step closer, my anger finally bubbles over. I'm sick of all his fucking bullshit. Riot is at my back. I can feel his heat through my sweatshirt. And if I'm being honest, it's giving me some extra confidence to finally speak up.

"What is that supposed to mean? You are being so fucking dramatic, as usual, Ben. Grow the hell up, will you. This man will never want to be with you, no matter how much you crush on him. He can shag any fuck boy he wants, so why the hell would he lower his standards for you?" he bitches.

A laugh spills from Riot's mouth, and I turn my head to look at him in complete shock. Does he agree with Harry? My stomach tightens, and I try to step away from him, but his arm wrapping around my waist stops me. Harry's gaze drops to where his hand is resting on my hip. The heat from his palm sears through my clothing and settles on my skin.

"Listen to me, you dull fuck. Ben is worth a hundred of you. He is loyal to a fucking fault. All my life I have fucked men of your status, which, by the way, is very fucking low on the totem pole."

I wince at Riot's words. I know he's shagged a ton of men over the years but hearing him say it doesn't sit well in my head. When I shuffle my feet to try and move away, Riot grips me tighter, keeping me in place.

"No fucker is higher than Ben, and now that I have him in my life, my bed, and on the back of my bike, my standards will be higher than ever, because he makes every cunt like you look like a weasel in bed." Riot leans forward, lowering his voice. "Oh, and doesn't his lips feel good wrapped around your cock? Fuck me, the best I've ever had." We stand there, Riot smirking at Harry, who looks stunned with his wide eyes and gaping mouth.

65

In a flash, he snaps it shut and turns his gaze to me, and I see fire. He is pissed.

"So you did cheat. You piece of shit. I always knew you were just like the scum of the club. I don't know why I wasted my time on you," he snaps.

This time, I step forward, and he backs up again, fear showing in his wide eyes.

"The men in that club are the most loyal and protective men you will ever meet. Family and friends mean something to them. As for me cheating, you broke up with me when you ran like a little pussy when three—yes, three fucking—men beat me the hell up. You did this, you sad piece of overdramatic fake queen."

I'm breathing heavily while I glare down at Harry, who is shorter than me. My chest is heaving, palms twitching to wrap around this man's throat, and not in the good way. I want to strangle the life out of him.

"You heard the man. Now fuck off. Leave," Riot snarls, stepping forward.

Harry gasps, before spinning on his shiny, booted heels and rushing down the driveway to his waiting car.

Once he's out of sight, I let out a breath and sigh with relief. Bending at the waist, my hands rest on my knees, and I breathe in and out deeply. Fuck me that was needed.

A hand runs up and down my back, soothing me. I shiver from the touch, knowing it's Riot. Why does he get to me so bloody much?

"Breathe, baby. He's gone." Hearing him call me 'baby' has me snapping into an upright position and glaring at him.

"Baby? Why the fuck are you all of a sudden calling me all these endearments, Riot? I have a face that you know; I have a fucking name that you know. So why the fuck are you still here taking care of me when all you want to do is fuck random people?" I snap. All the built-up anger is still lingering from Riot's earlier words, then the shit with Harry explodes.

I step away from him, but he doesn't let me go far. He grips my bicep, pulling me to him, and his lips slam against mine. His lips are soft, and his beard rubs against mine. His tongue invades my mouth, and I moan as his taste explodes across my taste buds.

Riot pulls me closer, his hard-on pressing against mine. He hisses, and I arch my hips, adding more pressure, making his grip on my arse tighten. My lungs scream for oxygen, but I don't break the kiss. This is something I've wanted for years, and it's finally fucking happening.

Riot rips his lips away before I'm ready for it, and I follow them, making him chuckle.

"Baby, if we carry on like this, I will fuck you out here for everyone to see, and I don't think you want that. Plus, when I fuck you for the first time, I want it in the privacy of your room, so I can take my time savouring every inch of your body." My heart skips a million beats as my body heats up and my cock turns to steel in my joggers.

Riot looks down between us and back up to my face with a smirk.

"Let's get you inside." I nod, my voice gone.

Fuck me, I've read enough romance novels to know how people feel when they get their first proper kiss with the one, they end up with, and sometimes I roll my eyes at the cheesiness of it, but fucking hell, I believe it now.

My heart is racing, my cock is throbbing, and my voice is no longer working as I watch this sexy man get my bags out of his car, smiling like he just ate the canary.

Holy fuck, am I the canary?

Pulling in a deep breath, I turn and head towards my front door, Friday right at my side. As soon as I unlock it and push it open, she runs into the house, sniffing, finding her scent like she always does.

I inhale deeply, wincing at the twinge in my ribs. I love the smell of my home; the lingering coconut smell from the battery-operated diffuser. Letting out a slow breath, I do a quick look around and see nothing is out of place.

"You, okay?" I startle at the sound of Riot's voice. I turn to face him, smiling.

"Yeah. It's so good to be home." I point to the bags he's carrying. "You can just put them over there by the small table. I'll sort them out later."

He nods and does as I tell him.

We stand there looking at each other for a few minutes, neither of us saying anything. Friday whines from her large bed, gaining our attention. Riot chuckles and walks past me to the back door. He opens it and Friday rushes out. Clearly, she needed to go.

I meet him in my kitchen, which I also love. It's my solace when I need to get out of my head. Cooking and baking helps me clear my head when I'm struggling with making the words flow.

My kitchen is very white and state of the art, but minimalistic. What can I say, I like things to be clean.

"She okay out there on her own?" he asks me.

"Yeah. She'll bark when she wants to be let back in." He nods at my explanation.

Again, silence settles between us. I bite my lip, making him growl, and he closes the distance between us, his hands landing on my hips. My dick jerks at the contact, and my balls become heavy with need for this biker.

"Biting that lip will get you in trouble, Ben."

His voice is deep, husky, and it makes my body respond to him. I shiver as his hand comes up and his thumb tugs my bottom lip free from my teeth. With his hand still touching my jaw, his gaze bores into mine.

"Let's get settled. We can order food and watch a film or something," he instructs. I nod and step away.

Riot being in my house is making the air statically charged with tension and sexual desire. Yeah, he has been here over the years with my brother, but he's never stayed any longer than necessary

I follow him down the short hallway, which has white walls and light wooden flooring, and some artsy items plotted around. Stepping into my living room, I see Riot already settled on my 'L' shaped cream sofa, his feet resting on my oak coffee table as he flicks through the channels on the wall-mounted TV. The two freestanding lamps, and the one basket lamp that sits in my fireplace because I don't use it, they cast a mellow glow across the room, giving it a romantic feel.

He looks up at me with a grin on his face.

"What do you fancy?"

You. Naked in my bed, letting me suck your dick, I think to myself, but refrain from saying it. I shake the thought, slip off my trainers before joining him on the sofa. We sit and flick through the TV guild looking for something to watch, then we order food. As the minutes tick by it gives me some time to organise my thoughts of what has been happening between Riot and me.

When the food arrives, we dig in, the conversation between us is light and easy, which is something I want out of a relationship. I know that Riot doesn't like drama in his life, so maybe this could work. If not, it will leave me broken and unable to come back from it.

Ten

Riot

Unbuttoning my jeans because my stomach feels like it's about to explode from all the Indian food I just ate, I breathe a heavy sigh and relax. Ben had the right idea today in wearing his joggers.

When I ordered food, I stripped out of my cut and t-shirt, then we settled down to watch *Black Panther*. I love that Ben is so passionate about a film franchise. To see this man get excited over something makes me happy. Seeing his face light up at certain scenes, or when he mutters the line, it makes me smile to see him happy. It also has me wanting to make him smile more and respond to me the way he does with these films.

He told me that the actor who played Black Panther died recently, and it's a damned fucking shame because he was epic. He played the character really well.

"Fuck, I am done. I don't think I can move an inch," I groan, making Ben laugh at me.

I cock an eyebrow at him, and he grins back.

"You can sleep here if you want. Take the guest room," he tells me.

Our gazes lock, and I groan as he bites his bottom lip out of worry over my answer. I know he can feel this off the charts chemistry between us. Fuck, it has been brewing for years, but as I've said, it was shit timing, so I held off and he pushed his feelings down when I let it be known that nothing was going to happen.

I know I need to make my intentions clear to him. He needs to know that he is mine in every fucking way.

"Baby, if I stay here, I won't be sleeping anywhere except in your bed with you," I tell him.

It's him who cocks an eyebrow this time. His cheeks are slightly flushed from the few beers we've had while eating and watching the film.

"I'm going to need you to explain this to me, Riot, because the mixed signals are fucking with my head," he says, looking down at the hand on in his lap.

"Hey, look at me. Come here, Ben." My voice is firm, letting him know I mean business.

He scoots over until our thighs touch. Even through the denim of my jeans, and the cotton of his joggers, I can feel the heat emanating from him in waves.

Hooking my hand around the back of his neck, I pull him to me until our noses almost touch. I can feel his hot breath wash over my face, and the feeling has my body standing to attention. My balls draw tight; the need to empty them grows the closer this man is to me.

With my free hand, I lift his leg and manoeuvre him so he is straddling me. He looks down at me with wide, dark eyes, letting me know he likes this. His hands go to my chest, my own going to his thighs, moving over the smooth material. My hands slide up further, over his hips, pushing the thin t-shirt up over his abs.

He gets my drift and pulls the t-shirt off, revealing how big his biceps are, something I've noticed more and more over the years. Ben takes pride in his body. He works out sometimes but mostly runs.

71

My gaze slides over his body, taking in the smooth skin and the planes of his abs and chest. He is fucking beyond perfect in my eyes. My hands follow my gaze, feeling his skin, and my cock gets harder and harder beneath his arse. I know he can feel it.

He grinds his body down, adding pressure to my cock.

"Fuck." My head slams into the back of the couch, making Ben smirk at me. "You think it's funny to make my cock hard, to have my balls tightening with the need to explode?"

His smirk morphs into a grin, which I return. He slides his hands up my chest and over my shoulders, feeling the muscles making me shiver. The smirk he gives me tells me he loves the effect he is having on me.

His eyes take in my body, causing my cock to swell in my jeans. While he is eye-fucking me, I do the same to him taking in every inch of his smooth skin. The way his muscles are defined, and his skin is flawless.

"You are so damned hot." His voice is husky, deep, proving he's as turned on as I am—that and the fact his joggers are fucking tented, his cock pointing at me from between his legs.

It is bad of me to love seeing his gaze roam over my body? Fuck no, I work out. I am damn proud of my body.

His eyes darken and his eyelids heavy with lust, and I know mine match his. Ben licks his lips, making me groan as I picture his mouth wrapped around my thick cock, his lips stretching around the girth.

"Fuck it," I mutter, before I snatch the back of his neck and bring his mouth down on mine.

Clearly, he wants it too because he meets my mouth with the same ferocity and desire, I'm giving him. His hands roam over my chest before moving up to wrap around my neck, holding me to him.

He gives a gentle rock of his hips, rubbing our dicks together, and I moan into his mouth. Fuck, he feels good. My tongue probes the inside of his mouth, stroking his, tasting the beer he's been drinking.

We kiss for Lord knows how long, our tongues playing for dominance, but I win every fucking time. I rule in the bedroom, something Ben will find out soon enough. When my lungs start screaming for air, I pull back and look at the man sitting on me. His breathing is harsh, his lips swollen.

I don't say anything at first, and neither does Ben. My body is buzzing from his touch, and my heart is beating like I'm about to have a fucking heart attack. As we catch out breaths, all I can think about is if my body is responding to him like this after just a kiss, fuck knows how my body and heart will cope when I finally get to fuck him, to feel his arse strangle my cock.

Licking my lips, I taste him on me, forcing me back for more. Leaning up, I kiss him again, but Ben pulls back, making me frown at him.

I watch as his tongues darts across his lips, his hands dropping from the back of my neck and resting on my stomach, making my muscles clench at the contact. Can't he move his hands lower and touch my cock; pull the fat fucker free?

"Kissing me doesn't give me the right idea of what you want, Riot. Don't get me wrong, the kiss was nice, but—"

"Nice? Mate, that's the best fucking kiss you will ever experience. Every kiss from me will be the best you'll ever have," I tell him with a straight face, but Ben breaks out in a smile then climbs off me.

Sitting on the coffee table in front of me, he rests his elbows on his knees, linking his fingers together and looking at his bare feet. I can see the cogs spinning in his head. My eyes twitch as I watch him and try to figure out what this is.

Shifting forward on the couch, I mirror his position, making sure my hands touch his.

"Look at me, Ben." I sigh and wait for him to do so. When he does, I carry on. "I know you think I'm a fucking whore, and yeah, you would be right, but not anymore."

He scoffs, looking to the side.

Hooking my finger under his chin, I turn his head back to me so he can look me in the eyes when I tell him this next part.

"For fucking years I have watched you grow up, knowing I couldn't touch you. Out of respect for your brother and mine, plus the club, I kept my distance. Shagging random men was the next best thing, besides the whisky. My drinking got bad when you started seeing men. It fucked with my head.

"I would get blind drunk, and my life went to shit. I know you remember the worst of it: when I woke up in bed with some naked chick. After that, I toned my drinking down, knowing that one day, hopefully, I would claim you. I had to prove to myself and to Mayhem that I was good enough. But then you started dating fuckface and it all went to hell. The fucking picked back up, though I managed to keep my drinking under control," I explain to him.

His eyes watch me intently, as he sits there not saying anything at first. He takes a deep breath then speaks.

"I'm proud of you for the drinking. I know first-hand what that can do to someone's body and mind. The mindless shagging was also a way of coping with whatever you were feeling, I get that. As for the naked chick, you messed up on that one, pal. But I am glad that you got it under control." he says, again looking away. He takes a few deep breaths before looking back at me.

"A good friend of mine had his heart broken and turned to the bottle. He stopped eating and lost so much weight. One night, he heard that his ex was out on date, so he got in

74

his car and drove over there to break it up. The alcohol caused him to lose control of the vehicle and he went over a bridge."

He shivers at the memory and I move in, pulling him onto my lap, and I have to say, I would say I like the way we fit, but fuck me, he's only inches shorter than me. I still love the feel of him there though.

"I'm sorry about your friend. When did this happen?" I ask, my hand resting on his mid-section, my thumb moving back and forth, causing his skin to break out in goosebumps.

"Last year," is all he says.

"Same age as you?" is my next question, and he nods. Fucking hell, what a waste. Ben is only twenty-five; too fucking young to die.

We sit like that for a while before he turns his head and kisses me. His kiss feels like he wants me to help him forget all the deep shit we just talked about, so I give him what he wants.

I will always give him what he wants and needs, because it's my job to make him happy.

His tongue invades my mouth as his breathing picks up, and his body gets hot. I like it rough and wild, and it seems my man does too. Breaking the kiss, I look at him, cupping his jaw to make him look at me.

"If this doesn't show you how much I want you, then I'm fucking everything up. I want you, Ben; in my life, in my bed, and on the back of my bike. I can't fucking wait to fuck you, to finally feel you wrapped around my cock." I jut out my hips, my cock making contact with his arse.

He moans deep in the back of his throat, and his eyes close. Yeah, he wants this. Without warning, I lower my hand and grip his dick. The hiss that leaves his mouth has my own damned cock leaking in my jeans.

"Fuck, you feel amazing. Big and thick. I can't wait to feel it slip into my arse as you fuck me." The words leave my mouth before I can stop them. I have only ever bottomed a handful of times, when I first started exploring my sexuality, but now I always top.

Ben pulls back and looks at me with wide eyes and a gaping mouth.

"Wait—what?" I just look at him, my own brain misfiring inside of my skull. Where the hell did that come from? "I assumed you topped. I mean, you've said it enough around the club, and there have been many occasions when I've had to listen to men brag about sleeping with you," he tells me.

Scrubbing my hands over my face, I take a deep breath and look at him.

"Listen, Riot. You don't have to say shit like that to convince me you're only going to sleep with one person. I mean—"

"Do I look like the type of bloke who blows smoke up someone's arse just so I can fuck them?" He shakes his head at me. "Good. And I'm not doing that to you. As for only sleeping with one person, yes, it is fucking true. I'm a man of my word, Ben. You know that, babe. So, when I say you're mine, do you honestly think I will go out and shag some random cunt when I have you waiting for me? Years, fucking years, I have waited for this," I gesture between us, "to happen. I am not going to throw it the fuck away. Get that through that big, smart head of yours."

I hold his gaze while he thinks over what I just told him. As the seconds tick by I start to feel a little uneasy. He grins at me and moves in for a kiss, his tongue licking my lips then delving into my mouth. After fuck knows how long, he pulls back, looking me dead in the eye.

"Just remember something, Riot. I write crime and thriller books for a living, which means hours upon hours of research. I know thousands of ways to kill you and make sure no one finds your body."

Can a man say dark shit like that to you with a sweet smile on his face? Hell yeah, they can, because my man just did, and I have to say, I am both scared shitless and fucking turned on at the same time.

Eleven

Ben

Taking a sip of my coffee, I never take my eyes off the screen in front of me. I'm finishing up my book, writing the epilogue. Every book needs an epilogue, otherwise it feels unfinished to me.

It's been a week since I locked myself away from the world to finish, and I have to say, I am bloody proud of myself. I even plotted out the next two books in the series and started looking into writing my very own MC series. Apparently, it's a hot genre to be involved in right now, so I might as well try my hand at it, since my very own brother is in a club.

And my man—maybe.

To be honest, I have no fucking clue what we are. He made this grand speech about us, but that was a week ago and I haven't heard from him nor seen him since. Though I locked myself away from the world, I still communicated with my family and friends. I waited three days then sent him a text, and I got nothing back. Zilch. Nix. Nada.

I refuse to ask Mayhem about it because I know he will either take the piss out of me for being clingy or have a go at Riot for not contacting me, and I don't want either of those things to happen. He made the prospect of us being together sound final, like a forgone conclusion, then upped and left in the middle of the night, not leaving so much as a note in his wake, then ghosted me for a week. Yeah, that's not going to work for me.

I buried myself in my book and planning, which helped take my mind off him most days, but during the nights he seeped back into my thoughts and ruled my mind. Arsehole.

My fingers once again fly over the keyboard, the words appearing fast across the screen. I've always been a fast typist, but that often means mistakes are made, so I'm thankful for my editor and proof-reader, who pick up my mistakes and call me on some of the random bullshit I write. They make my work readable.

As my character talks about finding their happy ever after, even after the kidnapping, torture, and killing of the men who took her, I can't help but smile. People out there do find love, and they do survive after living through such an ordeal.

Love conquers all, though so does a good doctor and money.

I smile to myself as my stomach tightens, as I close in on those sexy two words that every author loves…*The end.*

I slam my hands down on the table, making my coffee mug jump. Thank fuck it's almost empty. Friday barks, and I smile and jump up, startling her again.

She jumps up, pressing her two front paws on my chest, and we dance around on the spot like a pair of loons, but I don't fucking care, because I just finished my twenty-fifth book, bitches.

"We did it, girl. We bloody well did it. Thank fuck, huh?"

"I told you he would go crazy from only having that dog for a friend." My dad's deep voice startles me, and I let out a very unflattering, girly yelp.

Spinning around with my hand on my chest, I scowl at my parents, who are standing by the door smiling at me.

"You bloody scared me," I tell him, trying to catch my breath.

Friday leaps over to my parents, licking their faces when they fuss over her. They joke that she's my only friend, but they treat her like a grandchild, spoiling her and taking her on holidays to their caravan with them. Hey, each to their own.

"From the stupid dancing, can we assume you've finished, or have you truly gone loopy?" Mum asks.

I cross the room and hug her, then kiss her cheek, before hugging my dad.

"I have finished. Thank God," I sigh, my smile going nowhere.

"So, break time for you then, son. You taking the full two weeks this time?" Dad cocks his bushy eyebrow at me in question, because I always say I'm going to take a two-week break, but I get stir crazy and give in and start a new book.

We move into the living room after making some tea and coffee, each taking a seat. Friday curls up next to my mum and places her head in her lap.

"I'm taking the full two weeks. That book fried my brain. Plus, with everything that happened, I need to destress."

Speaking of destressing, I think of Riot, imagining him making me come so fucking hard I forget who and where I am. Making my body go lax and sink into the mattress, my muscles like jelly. A strong orgasm can remove the tension from your body because the endorphins rush through your blood, giving you a natural high and pain relief, making you relax and enjoy.

My dick stirs beneath my shorts, so I cross my ankle over my knee to hide the sudden bulge. This man is getting to me, getting under my skin, yet he hasn't really done anything to me.

"I'll believe it when I see it, Benny boy," Dad cracks. Mum slaps his arm playfully, making him smile.

I watch them together and think of how I want that. My parents are the complete opposite. They are both retired now. Mum used to work in a library, and Dad worked in a garage. He still owns it but has a manager run it for him. It got to the point where he couldn't get under the cars because of his knees. It was while helping Dad in the garage that Mayhem got his love for cars, and then Riot when they became friends.

"I'm sticking with it, Dad. This attack has made me see that I need to live more. That night could have ended so much worse for me, so I need to take my breaks and enjoy them. My world is writing, yes, but my life doesn't need to revolve around it," I tell them, and they both smile at me, showing their pride. But I also see fear in Mum's eyes as my words sink in of the night ending a different way coming true.

That is something that they always preach to Mayhem and me, that they are proud of us as men, and as human beings, because they brought us up, or if you ask dad, he dragged us up.

When I was laid up in Riot's room, I had some time to think. I looked back on my life and realised that yes, I have lived a full one, but I still have so much to do. I've only ever flown to Europe, but I have always wanted to visit America—LA and Miami mainly.

There was a short time when I thought Harry was the one for me. That quickly changed, but I didn't find the power to leave him until recently. Then I thought Riot would step up and tell the club—hell, the world—I'm his, but look how that turned out. I know how the club works, so I know he is on a run right now, but Mayhem, Chaos and Psycho still contact their old ladies when they're away.

"That's good to hear, son. Me and your mum were talking about popping down to the caravan; thought we'd take this little lady down with us so you can do things without worrying about her being locked up in the house all the time," Dad says, and Mum nods.

"Sounds like a plan. Thanks. We all know how much she loves the beach."

"Oh, we'll get some fish and chips and some ice cream, won't we, Friday? Yes, we will." Mum always speaks to my dog in a baby voice. Hell, she still speaks to Logan like he's a baby, and he's almost five.

I laugh. "Mum, the last time you gave her fish and chips her farts stank the house out for weeks."

"Oh, but she loves them, don't you, sweet pea?" She cups Friday's face and touches their noses. Dear Lord.

I take a sip of my tea, watching Mum fuss over my dog. It makes me happy because I know I can't give her grandchildren in the traditional way—not that it bothers either of my parents. They just enjoy seeing their two sons happy.

My phone beeps, making my heart skip a beat. I look at the device on the coffee table like it will suddenly turn into a Decepticon and attack me. I blink a few times, then reach over for it.

Riot's name is sitting there in the middle of my screen. I stare at it, not sure if it's a brush off or a poor excuse for not contacting me for days. Ignoring my parents bickering about what to feed Friday, I swipe my thumb across the screen and open the message.

Riot: Hey.

I blink, one, twice, and re-read the text. 'Hey' is all he sends me after days of ghosting me? What the fuck? I lock my phone and put it on the cushion next to me, then focus on my parents.

"Mum, just don't feed her the fish batter, and please, for the love of God, do not give her faggots and peas. She makes the house stink for weeks after eating that." I fake gag because it's true.

The last time Friday ate that crap, she farted for days. I spent a fortune on air fresheners. Fucking stinking-arse pooch.

My parents laugh at me as my phone vibrates, signalling a new text from Riot.

Dad looks at me, then my phone, then back to me.

"Do you need to get that?"

"Nope," I say, and he cocks an eyebrow at me. Sighing, I pick it up and open the text.

Riot: You read my text but didn't reply. Why?

Me: Didn't feel like it, just like you didn't feel like texting or calling all week. But then you do decide to grace me with a fraction of your time, and all I get is 'Hey'. If it's too much of a hassle to text, then please don't.

His reply is instant.

Riot: I'm on a run. Just busy.

Me: Busy? That's a shitty excuse, but whatever. My brother had time to text Lizzie. Just saying. Go and do club shit, Riot. My parents are here and we're *busy*.

I hit send and set my phone back down. My bratty side came out during that text, and I know it. It's something Mayhem always calls me on when shit doesn't go my way, and the side I'm not fond of when it comes out. He says it's my gay flare that appears, though I do try to stop it.

I never used to be like this, but after being around gay men for years, I picked up on a few traits and mannerisms.

83

"Why are your boxers in a twist? Is it Harry? Did you two get back together and now he's back to his old tricks again?" Mum asks me, looking concerned.

Babs Miller is a force to be reckoned with. She's a fierce mama bear when she needs to be, but sweet as pie when she likes you.

"It wasn't Harry," is all I say. I'm not sure if I should tell them about Riot. They have known about my crush for years, and they supported me and told me I needed to be sure he's what I want. If he was, they would support me. But they also told me to be careful around him because he's a freaking slut and could demolish me.

Sighing, I look at them both, relaxing into the couch.

"It was Riot." Both sets of eyes widen in shock, then they smile at me. Mum looks giddy. "Since I got beat up, he's been there for me, taken care of me, made offhand comments about me and him, and wasted my time. He kissed me and stayed the night, but then he left." I take a breath and let that information sink in with them, then I continue.

"He's been gone for a week, and I haven't heard from him until now. He says he was busy due to club business, and while I understand that, Mayhem text Lizzie, and he's with Riot. All his text said was 'Hey'. What the hell is that? Clearly, he's regretting making such bold statements about us and is letting me down slowly. Though can you let someone down if you haven't really started anything? Fucking hell, this man has me all twisted up and we aren't even a thing. I need a drink."

I get to my feet and head for the kitchen then pour myself a cheeky whisky and throw the sucker back.

The liquid burns the back of my throat and travels down to my belly. I take another shot as my parents walk into the kitchen.

"Ben, slow down, honey." Mum steps close to me and removes the bottle and shot glass from my hands.

84

Sighing, I rest my palms on the kitchen counter and close my eyes, pulling in deep breaths. How can this man have such a profound effect on me? I've known him for years and crushed on him most of my life, but fuck me, he shows me an ounce of interest and I go all gooey and fucked in the head at the same time.

"Son, you know how busy they get when it comes to club business. And try to remember this is all new to Riot. Cut the guy some slack, yeah?" Dad tells me.

"Maybe," is all I say, and go about putting the kettle on, but Mum stops me. Looking down at her short frame, I can't help but smile at her.

"Why don't we take you out for lunch, hmm? A place where Friday can come with us."

"Maybe down the Cliffs. They allow dogs in the garden out back," Dad adds.

"Okay, let me go and get changed," I tell him, then dart into my living room to pick up my phone before rushing upstairs.

I see I have three texts from Riot and hold my breath. Fuck, I'm like a teenage girl, for crying out loud.

Riot: Yeah, busy. Mayhem is a lazy fuck. That's why he's had the time. For fuck's sake, this is new to me, Ben. I've never had to text someone before. I usually just do my own shit.

Riot: So you're just going to ignore me. Fucking mature, Ben.

Riot: Fuck. Listen, I'll come around when I get back. We can talk more then.

Sitting down on my bed, I read over his texts and think of a reply. Should I be snarky or reasonable? Fuck, this is new to

85

me too, when it comes to him. I usually know the type of man I'm with, but Riot is so bloody unpredictable.

Me: It doesn't take long to send a text, Riot. I'm sorry that me wanting to know if you're okay, or even alive, is such a fucking inconvenience for you.

I hit send and get to my feet, pulling open drawers to find a nice pair of jeans and a long sleeve top to wear. When my phone beeps again, I quickly pick it up.

Riot: You worried about me, baby? I like that. We'll talk when I get back. Should be another day or so. Think of me when you're in bed, naked, with your hand wrapped around that fat cock of yours. Picture my hand there, wanking you off until you come over both of us.

Boom. My cock is hard.

Shit. Have I got time to rub one out before we go to lunch? Fucking sexy-arse biker, with his big muscles, fat cock and strong jawline.

Me: You wish. But I am hard as a fucking rock right now. I'm standing in my bedroom wearing just my boxers, getting ready to go to lunch with my parents, and all I want to do is rub my cock while thinking of you, and call out your name when I come.

Smiling proudly to myself, I set my phone down to get dressed. I pull on my dark blue jeans and a long-sleeved red and white baseball-type shirt. After slipping my feet into a pair of trainers, I head back downstairs, tucking my phone into the back pocket of my jeans.

It beeps and I smile to myself, hoping I've got him all hot and flustered like he did me. But then again, this is Riot, and doesn't do shame. Pulling out my phone, I read his text.

Riot: I'm as hard as a fucking right now too, and my brothers, including yours, are looking at me like I've grown five heads because I'm smiling like a loon. And it's because of you. You make me smile, Ben. As for that last text, you fucking wait until I get home. That sexy arse will be bent over my knee while I spank it and then fuck it. Later, baby ☐

Well fuck me, there goes my dick getting harder again, along with my heart swooning.

Twelve

Riot

The van I'm driving is bouncing along the uneven road that leads to the port where we're dropping off the three cars, ready to board the ferry. The drugs and guns are safely stored inside.

I fucking hate being in a cage. I'd rather have my bike between my legs, the wind rushing over my body, giving me the freedom I need to clear my head. We've been gone for fucking days, and I haven't had time to wipe my arse, let alone send a text to Ben. Before we left, I had to make sure all the vehicles were ready to drive and were well secured.

We left the clubhouse and got only a few miles down the road before the tyre blew, so we had to stop to fix that. Then we hit massive fucking traffic because of an accident. Thank fuck no one was hurt badly.

The shitty fucking van I'm driving is falling apart. Literally. The back bumper fell off on the motorway, so I had to deal with that. Then I had to fucking fix the side mirror because that was falling off, and I know the police can pull you for that shit.

We use old, run-down vans because they look like workman's vehicles and don't tend to draw much attention. The cars we use are everyday size, again to not draw too much attention. The people who drive the cars onto the ferry and drive off at the other end are people who work for the buyers, so they deal with the consequences if shit goes down.

I pull onto a slip road a few miles out from the port and see the men who will take the cars and van off us tonight. Then it's back to the hotel for some hot food, a drink, and sleep.

"Hey, fucker, we're here." I punch Mayhem in the arm. He grumbles and gets out of the van.

My brothers pull up behind me, and we all get out. The prosect pulls in once everyone is parked and starts unloading our bikes for the ride back.

"You damage my bike, and it will be your head rolling on the motorway home. You hear me, prospect?" Psycho calls out to him. His eyes widen with fear, but he nods and does his job.

"You're a prick, you know that?" I say to him, and he gives me a sadistic smile. Shaking my head, I meet Mayhem at the front.

I watch as he hands over the keys to all the vehicles. With a stance that says we're not ones to fuck with, I scan the area, checking for any possible threat to me or my brothers. Even the fucks taking the cars from us. The one at the front of the group smiles at Mayhem and steps forward with a box I know is filled with cash.

"Always a pleasure working with the Road Wreckers MC," he states, handing over the box.

Mayhem nods and shakes his hand before stepping back. They make small talk about the cars and drugs they may be looking into selling.

"How's that handsome brother of yours, Mayhem? Please tell me he's finally single," the leader asks, and my spine goes steel straight.

My shoulders square off, and my heartrate picks up.

"Easy, brother," Psycho says from next to me in a low, calm voice. I nod, knowing he's right. Now is not the time to kick off. This guy and his boss provide a ton of money for the club.

Mayhem chuckles. "Sorry, man, but you missed out again."

"Damn. You need to call me the next time he's single. He's a looker, hot; I could do with spending some time with him between the sheets." His voice goes all dreamlike.

The suit he's wearing looks expensive. I know he could give Ben whatever he needs and could ever want, but I'm a selfish cunt. I won't be giving him up for anyone.

"The only man who will see Ben between the sheets is me," I snarl, my anger taking over.

I feel a hand on my arm and look down, then follow the arm and find it attached to Psycho. We glare at each other, before he finally lets go. He must see something in my eyes that tells him I won't do shit right now, but that doesn't mean something unfortunate won't happen to this fuck somewhere down the road.

"Is that so?" he asks and looks to my brother for confirmation. Mayhem nods, grinning. He's loving the fact that Ben is getting to me more than any other man has.

"Very fucking so. Ben is mine, and believe me, you're missing out. My man is…" I breathe in deep and moan, "a fucking god in bed." I smirk at him, my anger fading as the smile drops from his face.

"Mate, what the fuck? That's my brother you're talking about," Mayhem bitches, but I laugh at him.

"Get used to it, brother." I wiggle my eyebrows at him.

"When did this happen? I thought he was seeing that prancy-arse bitch from the drama club," the prick asks.

"That ended. Ben got the shit beat out of him and the prancy-arse bitch bolted; left him to take on three guys on his own," I explain. I watch as anger takes over his face, just like it did mine that night.

"Tell me you got the men who did it," he snaps.

Who the fuck does this guy think he is, asking about my man? Ben is mine to protect. I will end the cunts who hurt him, and believe me, Harry will get his, too, in every way he can without me killing the slug.

"Not yet, but we will. You have nothing to worry about, man. I'll get the wankers who hurt my man."

With that, I walk over to my bike and get on, firing my baby up. My brothers follow suit, Mayhem tucking the box into one of his saddle bags while the prospect starts up the club's van, waiting for us to pull out of the layby.

With every mile we ride, my thoughts are on Ben and the state he was in when he came to us that night; the way he looked in my bed; how he felt on my lap that last night at his house; the way his mouth felt against mine.

My dick thickens behind the zipper of my jeans, and I moan, thanking the road gods my brothers can't hear me.

It's not long before we're all pulling into the car park of the hotel we're staying in for the night. We always stay for one night, leaving a paper trail that indicates we were just out enjoying a bike ride.

As I park my bike, my brothers pull in next to me and get off their own bikes, before we all walk into the hotel's main entrance. We look like a fucking bunch of misfits, but we don't give a fuck. People sitting in the reception area and the bar that can be seen from the main door give us the side eye. The women tuck their handbags closer, making me smirk.

I wink at a group of older ladies who look like they're in town for a girl's weekend. They giggle and smile, and one even winks back.

"Oh, I'd like to ride a bad boy," one calls out, making me and the boys laugh.

"Sorry, ladies, I'm taken, and I don't think my man would be happy with me straying," I call back. Some people gasp, while others groan.

"Oh, bollocks. Why are all the hot ones taken or gay? Bugger." I can't help but laugh at that statement. I've heard it so many fucking times over the years.

Mayhem checks us in, and we all go to our rooms. I take a quick shower before joining the brothers down in the bar for a few drinks. Not too many. I don't need a hangover when I ride home tomorrow.

There are already drinks on the table when I get there. Mayhem is deeply engrossed in his phone, no doubt texting Lizzie. The same with Psycho. He's one quiet but mean motherfucker. You do not want to cross him in a dark alley, or anywhere, for that matter. He never says much, but when he does it usually makes sense and is usually filled with some dark crazy shit.

Pulling out my phone, I send a quick text to Ben.

Me: Hey.

I look at my phone, wishing it to chime like a teenage girl waiting on a text from her crush. What the hell? I see Ben has read the text, but he doesn't reply.

Me: You read my text but didn't reply. Why?

His reply is instant.

Ben: Didn't feel like it, just like you didn't feel like texting or calling all week. But then you do decide to grace me with a fraction of your time, and all I get is 'Hey'. If it's too much of a hassle to text, then please don't.

Me: I'm on a run. Just busy.

Ben: Busy? That's a shitty excuse, but whatever. My brother had time to text Lizzie. Just saying. Go and do club shit, Riot. My parents are here and we're *busy*.

Sighing, I take a pull from my beer before placing the bottle back down on the table. I look at the men around me and see they're all watching the game on the TV. Got to love a bit of football. I'm a Chelsea supporter myself, unlike Ben, who supports fucking Arsenal. But I suppose someone has to.

I reply to him, getting pissed that he's being a dick right now. I've been busy. He knows how club runs can get. He's been around the club long enough to know how things work.

Me: Yeah, busy. Mayhem is a lazy fuck. That's why he's had the time. For fuck's sake, this is new to me, Ben. I've never had to text someone before. I usually just do my own shit.

Me: So you're just going to ignore me. Fucking mature, Ben.

I sigh and run my fingers through my hair. This relationship shit is new to me. I don't want to piss him off, but clearly, I am.

Me: Fuck. Listen, I'll come around when I get back. We can talk more then.

Ben: It doesn't take long to send a text, Riot. I'm sorry that me wanting to know if you're okay, or even alive, is such a fucking inconvenience for you.

When I run my hand through my hair, it gets the attention of Mayhem. He looks down at my phone and frowns.

93

"Ben?" he asks, and I nod. "He pissed you're only now texting him?" I nod again and he chuckles.

"How did you know?"

"Lizzie." He shrugs and it's my turn to nod.

Looking down at my phone, I smile, sensing he cares about me, what with his worrying that I might get hurt while on club business. I type out a reply, a grin forming on my face.

Me: You worried about me, baby? I like that. We'll talk when I get back. Should be another day or so. Think of me when you're in bed, naked, with your hand wrapped around that fat cock of yours. Picture my hand there, wanking you off until you come over both of us.

Ben: You wish. But I am hard as a fucking rock right now. I'm standing in my bedroom wearing just my boxers, getting ready to go to lunch with my parents, and all I want to do is rub my cock while thinking of you, and call out your name when I come.

Holy mother of cunts.

My dick goes rock hard, and I'm pretty it's fucking weeping at his words. This is the author side of him coming out because he knows how to turn his fucking readers on with his sexy words.

My smile widens and I look up when I feel eyes on me. All my brothers are grinning at me because they know what the fuck is going on. Hell, we've all ribbed the brothers who have old ladies over the sexting they do.

Shaking my head, ignoring the slight warmth that now fills my cheeks, I reply to my man, getting him just as worked up as he's made me.

Me: I'm hard as fuck right now, and my brothers, including yours, are looking at me like I've grown five heads because I'm smiling like a loon. And it's because of you. You make me smile, Ben. As for that last text, you fucking wait until I get home. That sexy arse will be bent over my knee while I spank it and then fuck it. Later, baby □

Pocketing my phone, I finish off my beer and order more for me and the boys. We drink, talk and rib each other over random shit, then go outside and spark up a cigar, which is my favourite thing to end the night with. A glass of whisky and a cigar relaxes me and helps me sleep.

This is the life I love. Freedom, loyalty, respect, and love.

Thirteen

Ben

Closing my laptop, I rub my eyes with the heel of my hand, hoping to make them see straight. I've been proofreading for the last four, maybe five hours, adding to my latest book and checking for any errors before I sent it off to my beta readers, then my editor.

Pushing my chair back, I get to my feet then stretch my back out. It clicks and feels amazing after being seated for so long. Not a good idea to work at the dining table, but that's the life of an author that many don't see. The struggles we face, the body issues we have to deal with.

Friday whines and walks over to the back door, telling me she wants to go outside. Stepping over to her, I pull the door open, and she bolts for her favourite tree at the bottom corner of the garden.

Taking a page out of her book, I pad over to my downstairs toilet to relieve my screaming bladder. With the amount of tea and water I've consumed today, I'm surprised I haven't been pissing every five minutes.

Once I've finished, I wash my hands and make my way back into the kitchen to make a snack, but the ringing of my doorbell stops me. Frowning, I walk back through the house, towards the front door. Pulling it open, I'm surprised to see

Riot leaning against the small porch frame I had built a year or so ago.

"Hey, I brought food," he says, and pushes past me into the house.

I stand there, stunned at his sudden arrival. When we messaged the other night, he went silent on me again. That was three nights ago, he was only supposed to be away for a day or two.

"Um, hello. Why are you here?" I call to him as I follow him into my kitchen.

He sets a bag of containers on the kitchen island, then starts opening cupboards—looking for plates, I assume.

"I told you, I brought food and beer," he says without looking at me.

I watch as his t-shirt pulls tight across his biceps as he reaches up to pull open the small cupboard doors. His jeans hug his fine arse, which I would love to get my hands on.

Nope, not happening.

I'm not playing games with him. He's either in or he's out. My head and heart can't take this ghosting shit game he's playing. I thought when he told me he wanted me that he was being genuine—hell, he looked and sounded genuine—but his performance over the last few days says otherwise.

"Here," I sigh. I pull out two plates from the correct cupboard and place them on the island, then step around him, my hand brushing against his thigh. I feel him tense and look up at him, seeing his eyes darken. His beard is a little longer, and I have to say, I like it.

I take out some cutlery from the draw and set them next to the plates, trying my best to ignore the way his penetrating gaze is burning into my body

"What did you get?" I ask, as I start pulling the containers out. The scent of the Kung Pao chicken hits my senses and I moan.

Damn I love this meal.

97

Next is boiled rice and some chips. Nice to know he likes half and half. I remove the two bags, one with prawn crackers in and the other a bundle of poppadom's.

Damn, this man likes to eat, but then again, he uses the gym at the club a few days a week and works hard, so he needs the calories.

Heat hits my bare back, reminding me that I'm only in running shorts. What can I say, I like to be comfortable when I work. His big hands rest on my hips, his calloused palms rough on my skin.

I stand stiff in front of him when he leans in closer. A shiver races over my body as I feel the hairs of his beard against my shoulder, then his soft lips. He kisses me there then moves closer to my ear, before taking the lobe between his teeth.

My cock reacts to the touch, tenting the thin material of my shorts. I moan as he kisses across my bare skin, making goosebumps appear in favour of his touch. He presses into me harder, his hard dick pressing into my arse cheeks.

My hips involuntarily push back against him, making him growl into my ear. My eyes flutter closed at the sensations that flash all over my body.

His kisses to my neck become harder, his teeth nipping at the sensitive skin. I arch my head to the side, giving him better access.

"What about the food?" I pant out.

"Fuck the food," he growls.

"I'd rather fuck you," I reply.

He snarls behind me, pressing his cock into my arse even harder. Suddenly, he bends me over the top of the island, and the cold marble top makes my nipples pebble.

His hands swoop down and cup my arse cheeks, before he grips them tightly in his palms, his fingers flexing against my flesh. My cock jerks, hitting the island in front of me. Riot leans over my back, his leather cut rubbing against my skin. I can feel the difference between the leather and the club patches.

"Do not tempt me, Ben. I want you in more ways than I have anyone else. You've had me hard whenever you're around. Just the thought of you makes my cock become like steel. No other fucker before you has ever satisfied me. They were a tight hole to fuck until I got you."

His words should piss me off, and in way they do, but he was single. He could fuck whoever he wanted. Besides, I was shagging my boyfriends.

"Then why don't you?" I pant, my own arousal building. The need to come is driving me crazy.

I'll let this man do anything he wants to me, as long as he makes me come and cries out my name when he does.

"Fuck," he mutters. Then he's pulling me up and round to face him before he slams his mouth down on mine.

The kiss is hard, fast, and frenzied, and I love it. I don't always need soft. I'll take whatever the moment needs. Kissing is my thing. Harry hated it; he said it was childish to kiss each other all the time, especially in public.

Will Riot be like that? Shit, I hope not. I want to scream from the rooftops that this man is mine. If he is mine, that is.

"Wait. Stop." I regretfully break the kiss to look him in the eyes.

"What is it? I thought you wanted this as much as I do?" he asks, his voice deeper, sexier than his usual tone.

We stare at each other, catching our breaths. Once my stupid heart is beating at a normal pace, I gesture between us and ask, "What is this?"

Riot frowns. His gaze drops to our dicks, which are bulging and proud. With a cocked eyebrow, he looks back up at me, a smirk now plastered on his lips, making me lick my own.

He grins, leaning in for a kiss, while one of his hands cups my hardened cock, giving it a squeeze. I moan into his mouth as he devours me like he's savouring me, committing me to memory.

The kiss goes on for Lord knows how long. I'm completely lost to him, completely at his mercy, and fuck me, I'm happy to be right where I am. His hand moves from my dick and rests on my hip as he leans in, rubbing his own hard dick against mine, making the both of us groan.

Pulling back, I break the kiss, my lungs screaming for air. I've written this in my books, but never have I ever experienced it before, not with Harry nor any other man I kissed before him.

We stand looking each other in the eye, his gaze telling me that he wants this as much as I do. His dark green eyes are fierce, and his lips are red and swollen from our kisses. Usually, I would feel uncomfortable looking a man in the eye this close, but Riot has this calming hold over me.

"This is real. Solid. I've waited way too fucking long to have you, and I'm not going to let you slip away and shack up with some pansy-arse bitch like Harry." His voice is gruff, deep, and sends a new wave of shivers through me, making my nipples hard.

They draw Riot's attention, and he grins at me. That grin has got him so much dick over the years. I know he's shagged a lot of men, and I bet it was that mouth that won them over every time.

"If we do this, Riot, then you're mine as much and I am yours. You want to fuck other men, there's the door." I wave my arm toward the exit. "You say you've wanted this for a long time, well so have I, and if you think I'll stand by and watch you cheat, then you have another thing coming."

I cross my arms over my chest, forcing Riot to take a small step back, though not far enough to miss the heat from him soaking into my skin. I stand strong, even though my cock and balls, along with my head, are begging for me to drop to my knees and worship his dick.

When he cocks an eyebrow at me, I notice how well trimmed they are. Most men wouldn't give a shit about something like that, but clearly Riot does. I have no doubt he manscapes, too, like I do. Some men like having a hairy lover, and I do too, to a certain extent. I don't fancy a mouthful of hair when I suck a man's dick or eat their arse. That's why I return the favour and shave everywhere, from the base of my cock down.

I'm forced to drop my arms to my sides when Riot's hands slip around my waist, trapping me between his hard body and the island behind me.

"No ifs, buts or maybes. I'll tell the club tomorrow. It's time I step up and claim what's mine. You good with that?" He looks deep into my eyes, and I nod, my voice stolen from me.

"Good," is all he says, giving me a sexy as hell smile. Then he drops to his knees.

His hands make quick work of pulling my shorts down, and I'm thanking God that I went commando today. Licking his lips, he grips my cock in his rough hand, grinning up at me, before he drops his gaze to my dick. When he pokes his tongue out and licks the head, I shiver. My hand goes to the back of his head, and the short hairs scratch against my palm. When I try to pull him closer, he fights me, then looks up with a salacious smile.

"I'm in charge, baby. Just because I'm on my knees for you, it doesn't mean you get to control me. This is me showing you what you mean to me. I do not, and I mean never, get on my knees for anyone."

His words hit me square in the chest.

With his gaze locked on me, he sucks the air out of my lungs when he sucks on the head of my cock.

"Fuck," I breathe out.

My head falls back as he completely swallows my dick. The head hits the back of his throat, pulling a growl from me, and my hand flexes in his hair. I want to pull him onto me more, but I love the thought of him dominating me from his knees.

I watch as my cock slips into his mouth, past his red lips that are stretching to accommodate me. I'm bigger than the average man, but clearly Riot has no issues sucking me back.

"Fuck yeah. Harder," I pant out.

With my cock in his mouth, he looks up at me. The hairs from his beard slide across my sensitive shaft as he bobs his head up and down my cock.

The sensual feeling of him sucking me off while looking at me is something I haven't done before. I did try it with Harry, but he hated it, said it freaked him out. But with Riot, it's sexy and carnal.

"Oh shit," I call out as one of his hands cups my balls, pulling down on them, stretching the sack out, making the skin pull tight and sending waves of desire through me.

"You like that, baby?" he asks me, then licks my cock from base to head before harshly sucking on the swollen head.

"Yeah. More."

He winks, and then he's moving again. His mouth pulls me in, devouring me, pushing me closer and closer to my orgasm. A hand slides between my arse cheeks, one finger, then two, adding pressure to my arsehole.

My body shudders at the contact with the sensitive area, but then his fingers disappear. Looking down, I see him suck on the digits, getting them wet so he can slide them into me. He smiles at up at me as I watch him, before moving his finger back to my arse. He slides it in, pumping slowly at first, then takes my dick into his magical mouth once more.

"Fuck, that feels good," I pant out.

Erotic vibes pass between us as I move between breathing heavily and growling out my desire. He fucks my arse with his finger and swallows my cock. When his throat convulses around me, I see stars.

"I'm close." I grip his hair tighter and my knees lock in place, stopping me from collapsing to the floor.

His mouth sucks harder and his finger moves more roughly. When he touches the magic spot, my balls draw up, my spine tingles, and I explode, shooting my cum down his throat. His gaze locks on mine as he swallows every drop. I can't look away from him as he sucks slowly then licks the tip of my dick, making sure he doesn't miss any.

Nothing is said as he gets to his feet, his smile firmly in place on his handsome face. Not wanting to wait to feel his lips on mine again, I pull him to me. My lips press against his, tasting myself on him, and his tongue duels with mine, making him groan and pull me tighter to him.

His cock, still encased in his jeans, presses against my bare shaft. I want to feel him come for me, just like he made me come for him. I reach for his dick and squeeze, before rubbing my palm over him, but he pulls away before I can make my way to the button and zip.

"Not tonight. Tonight was all for you, to show you I want you and only you. I may be a dirty-mouthed biker with a rather unfavourable past, what with my lifestyle and sex life, but you're the one I want, and I will have you. No backing out now, babe."

His voice holds so much promise, so I nod. Believing his words. His smile is enough to put anyone on their arse, but he's all mine. His smiles, smirks and grins are all fucking mine, and I will cut a bitch if they try to get between us.

Fourteen

Riot

Walking into the clubhouse after spending the night with Ben, I feel like I'm on cloud fucking nine. Even though I didn't fuck him last night, just being with him, holding him, was nice. It felt right. Call me a fucking pussy all you want. I don't give a fuck what people think of me.

If I cared what people thought of me, I would be rocking in the corner of a mental institute by now, drugged up to the eyeballs, or dead from suicide. No fucker has any right to say shitty things to people. We all live different lives. That's what makes the world a beautiful place: the colours, the sizes, the different personalities.

I've said it once and I'll say it again: if we were all the same, the world would be a boring, mothering fucking place.

Walking over to the bar, I see Chaos frowning down at some papers. He never stops working, this man. This is why he's the best man to rule this club. He's the best kind of club president you will ever find.

"You okay, brother?" I ask, taking the stool next to him.

He sips from his coffee before placing the mug on the bar top and turning to look at me. Dark circles are prominent under his eyes, showing his lack of sleep. This man carries the world on his shoulders.

"Yeah, just sorting through club shit. Paperwork I am way fucking over. I'm sifting through the next lot of runs and making sure we have enough time to get it all done."

I slap him on the back. "We've got this, mate. No worries. You know me and the boys have your back and will get shit done. I bought three more vans, two bikes and a fucking tugboat. Between Mayhem, Psycho, and me, we can fix them all up to carry a shit ton of product. More than we have before."

He nods and studies me for a second, before he smiles, turning fully on his stool and resting his arm on the bar.

"Something is different with you."

"See something you like?" I jest with him, and the fucker laughs.

"What are you two cackling about like a pair of witches over here?" Mayhem says, cleaning the oil from his hands with a cloth as he walks over to us.

Those cloths can be found all over the fucking place; in the garage and the clubhouse. It drives the old ladies fucking crazy.

"Something is different with him. I think he looks almost fucking happy, or he just got laid really fucking good," Prez states. The two men look at me, and I can't keep the smile off my face.

This is all Ben's doing. He doesn't need to try to make me happy; just being with him does that.

Mayhem smiles wide, clicking his fingers and pointing at me.

"You went over to see my brother last night, didn't you?"

"I did." I wiggle my eyebrows and his smile fades. A fake gag soon follows.

"Oh shit, I do not want to hear about you and my brother fucking. Hell fucking no, bitch."

I laugh, and so does Chaos. Psycho joins us, cracking a small smile, which used to be unusual for him, but then he got together with Evie. I slap him on the back, looking him in the eye, then wink.

"Fuck off." He pushes me away from him, making me laugh harder.

"I need to call Church." I look at Chaos, who nods.

"Church, fuckers," he bellows into the room.

We all follow behind the man who runs this club, who leads us into war but always has our backs; the man who will do anything for his club and family.

We each take a seat around the large wooden table in the room we use for Church and wait for Prez to start the meeting.

"You called Church, brother. Say what you've got to say." Prez points to me and I nod.

"I'm claiming Ben Miller as my old man." I barely finish my sentence before the room erupts into cheers.

I get pulled out of my seat, and they all hug me and slap me on the back. The love and pride I have swells for this club. They accepted me when I told them I was gay years ago, but for them to accept that I'm claiming a man is beyond something I could ever ask for.

Not once have they ever showed their disgust toward my sexual preference because that is not what the Road Wreckers MC is about. We stand for equality and diversity.

You are who you are, and you love who you love.

"About time, fuckface." Mayhem pulls me in for another hug before we all take our seats again.

"For years I've carried feelings for him, but I held off out of respect for the Miller family and the club. When I saw the state he was in after the beating, it set my fire burning hotter. The riot in me built to a point it was ready to explode and find the fuckers who hurt my man. They need to be found."

"They will be. We have an idea about which members of this little crew did it. We just need to track the individuals down," Psycho tells me.

106

I nod at the man, knowing he's doing his best—hell, everyone in the club is. We've put feelers out to track these sacks of shit down, so hopefully we'll get them soon. I can't fucking wait to get my hands on their scrawny necks and watch as the life drains from their eyes.

My fists clench on my thighs as images of Ben's beaten body flash in my head, as I picture what those fucks did to him that night. Who the fuck gangs up one someone? I'll tell you who: a fucking coward. Someone who knows they can't stand up to someone on their own.

"Riot?" I blink and get out of my head, then look toward Mayhem.

"What?"

"How is Ben? I haven't talked to him in a few days. My mum mentioned something about him being jumpy when she was with him."

I frown. This is the first time I'm hearing about this. I think back to the times I've spent with him since the beating. He never seemed jumpy with me. He was always relaxed and at ease.

"He hasn't said anything. He seems okay when I'm with him," I explain, and they nod. "I'll talk to him."

"Good. Now, on to the money making, brothers," Chaos pipes up.

"I'm on loan runs tomorrow, collecting for this month, and catching up on the pigs who missed a few payments," I tell Prez, who nods.

"I bet you're wanting to get that frustration out on said pigs." Mayhem grins widely at me.

"Yeah—unless, you know, Ben is doing it for you," Tracker adds.

"Mate, come the fuck on. I don't want to hear that shit." Mayhem throws his lighter at him.

We all erupt into laughter, but he gripes under his breath, "For your information, and to settle this cry baby over here, I haven't fucked Ben yet. I sucked him off, but no fucking." I wiggle my eyebrows at Mayhem, who flips me off.

I love fucking with him, but I respect the hell out of him, and I know he respects me. If he didn't, he wouldn't be happy with me being with Ben. Not that it would stop me from claiming him, but having the club's blessing would have gone a long way. Seeing Ben hurt made me wise up to my feelings. He is mine no matter what.

"Okay, fuckers, is there any other gossip you want to get off your chests?" Prez asks the room.

We all shake our heads, and Prez nods.

"Okay, let's get shit sorted. We have a ton of business to go over, and I have my woman waiting for me at home, ready and wet." He grins, before jumping right into club business.

We talk over the idea of adding to our current orders, possibly opening up some legit businesses, and discuss outsourcing to help find the pricks who hurt Ben. When Prez ends Church, I leave the room with the rest of the men and make my way out to my section of the garage. I need to finish up on the bike I'm repairing.

"Brother, can I have a word?" Mayhem calls to me.

I turn to face him and nod. "Go for it."

His face is pensive, giving me the vibe that this is going to be a serious conversation, not just some brothers goofing off. This is an older brother looking out for is younger brother.

He sighs and starts. "I know how you feel about Ben. I've seen it for years. Did I like seeing you with other men, knowing you had feelings for my baby brother? Fuck no, but I understood where you were coming from. You weren't ready to settle down. You liked to shag around like the slut you are. I had to bite my tongue so many fucking times over the years when it came to you and Benny Boy, because they're your lives to live.

"Now that you've claimed my brother, if I see you show any interest in another man, I will gut you. You'll not only

108

lose that sausage you have swinging between your legs, but I will dig your eyes out with a dirty spoon and place them in a jar at my house. So, man to man, brother to brother, I'm telling you that if you hurt my blood brother, I will spill your blood, you hear me?"

We stand in a face off, Mayhem in a defensive stance with his arms crossed over his chest, legs wide. Me, I have my thumbs hooked in the belt loops of my jeans, my hip slightly cocked as I stand with my legs apart, showing a relaxed posture.

"So, you think my dick is big enough to swing between my legs?" I ask him.

"Fuck you, you prick. That's all you took from that?" he asks, grinning at me.

"Listen, man. I know where you're coming from. I won't hurt Ben. No threat or warning will change that. Call this a hallmark fucking moment; I don't give a shit, Ben is mine, and I will do everything in my power to love and protect him. You know I'm a man of my word."

He nods and moves in to hug me, slapping his hands on my back, and I return the action.

This man is my brother in heart and soul. We have been through so fucking much together over the years, done some stupid, crazy shit, but in the end we did it side by side.

It was always Mama Babs who stepped in to help us out, her feisty mouth all stacked up in her pint-size frame.

"Alright, mate, I'm out." With that, he goes to leave the room.

"Oh, and I *was* a slut, fuck you very much," I call out as he leaves the garage.

He flips me off over his shoulder, making me laugh. Once I've calmed down, I get to business, prepping shit ready for the new product to be added. Then I have to do my collection rounds, which is something that costs me my time, but it brings the club a lot of money.

Fifteen

Ben

Leaning my forearms on the handle of my shopping trolley, I look down at the list in my hand, which tells me I need to pick up a lot of chicken and red meat, along with rice, pasta, and vegetables.

I have huge issues with snacking. #authorproblems

We have to sit and write for hours at a time, and we sometimes forget to eat, so we snack on something easy to reach for. It's the reason I do three workouts a week and run most mornings. It helps with the extra calories and helps clear my head when I'm deep in a story.

I add a huge bag of pasta to the trolley, then move on to the next item. My phone chimes from my pocket, so I fish it out, looking down at the notification. I click on it, and it takes me to Instagram, where I see a silly photo of Logan wearing a pair of plastic glasses and a brightly-coloured wig.

Smiling, I let out a chuckle as I type out a comment, telling Lizzie he looks amazing. He's a crazy kid and I love him with all my being. Logan is the best little boy ever; funny and quirky. He and has a serious side that makes us adults laugh.

Pocketing my phone, I move on to the meat section of the supermarket, avoiding the fish section because the smell makes me gag. I place some fresh steaks in the trolley, then move down to the lean turkey mince so I can make some mini cottage pies that I load up with vegetables.

"Well, look who it is. The man who likes to use men." I stiffen at the sound of Harry's annoying voice.

Turning around, I see him standing there with another bloke, who's dressed just like my ex: tight jeans that look like they were painted on his stick-thin legs; a random, colourful t-shirt that looks baggy on him; and some black, shiny sandals. His hair is perfect, as is his make-up.

"Still being dramatic as ever, Harry." I sigh, turning to face them head on, and don't miss the way the other man looks me over.

"Oh, you know I love the dramatics, Ben. At one time so did you. I mean, how many times did you bitch, whine and moan over that scummy biker shacking up with someone?"

I suck in a breath, my jaw clenching at him bringing Riot up.

"Fuck off, Harry. Riot is not a scummy biker. He may be dirty in bed, but he's definitely not scummy." His eyes go wide at my words, and I smirk at him.

Yeah, he gets what I just said. A creepy smile slides over his face as he slips an arm around the man's waist, pulling him closer. He reaches up and kisses his cheek, and they look at each other smiling. When they both look back at me, I see Harry's eyes narrow w slightly, like he sees that this display doesn't bother me. I'm not jealous of him moving on. Hell, I have.

"The thing with you, Ben, is that you're boring. You never like change, so you will never advance in the love department. You will be a sad, lonely, old gay man who writes mediocre books, that again will get you nowhere." He smiles proudly at the thought he's knocked me down a peg, but bloody hell his words mean nothing.

I am over his bullshit ways and words, he is nothing to me anymore.

"I may be sad, lonely and boring, but at least I'm not a fucking fake. A coward," I snap back.

"If you say so, *Benny boy*." Harry grins at me, and so does his boyfriend.

"I do actually. I—"

"There you are, babe. I told you to wait for me." I get cut off by Riot's voice.

I look over my shoulder and see him striding toward me. The heavy boots he's wearing thud across the floor. His jeans are snug against his thighs, leading up to his narrow waist, and the green t-shirt under his leather jacket is tight across his stomach.

My mouth waters at the sight of him, as well as my cock chubbing out in my own jeans. He grins at me and closes the gap between us, then takes my mouth in a searing kiss that literally steals my breath. His hand slips around my waist, pulling me to him, and the other hand grips the back of my neck.

He kisses me long and deep while his tongue toys with mine.

Someone clears their throat, but we don't stop kissing. Nope, Riot stops only when he wants to stop. They cough louder, making Riot grin against my lips. Pulling back, he smiles down at me.

"Hi," I breathe.

"Hey, baby," he replies.

"Of fucking course you run to him. You had to pay him to pretend to be with you, Ben. He has never wanted you, and he's clearly using you now. Grow the fuck up. This is pathetic," Harry snarks off, waving his hand dramatically in our direction. In answer, my hackles rise.

113

"Fuck you, Harry. I didn't pay him. We're together, thanks to you. You bolted and he was there to help me heal. He stood by me, unlike you."

"Oh whatever. You're dreaming again, as usual." He looks at Riot. "By the way, we were talking. How rude of you to interrupt," he whines like a petulant child, even cocking his hip out to the side.

How the hell did I ever find this man attractive? He's a spoilt child and is proud of it. He has never done a hard day's work in his life. He expects everything to be handed to him because he's gay.

That is the way he's always thought. He thinks gay men and women are owed so much because they've taken a social beating over the years. Yet that's not true. Yes, there has been violence—hell, there always will be—but more and more people are accepting of sexual preference these days. Just because you're gay, it doesn't mean you can be mean or act like a child.

"I didn't hear any talking. I heard a bunch of babbling going on, like an excited toddler learning how to speak, but no actually adult conversation coming through." Riot replies, turning to face the two other men but keeping me close to him, his arm firmly around me.

His hand on my hip flexes, making my dick turn from a semi to rock fucking hard in seconds.

"Excuse me? Who the hell do you think you are? You can't talk to me like that," Harry chimes back in a high-pitched voice, while clinging to the new boyfriend.

Fuck, his voice really is annoying.

"I can say and do whatever the hell I want, fuckface. And I don't give a flying fuck who you are, but yes, I do know you—unfortunately." I watch as Harry blanches and almost takes a step back. Riot looks at his boyfriend.

"You with him?" The man nods, looking scared as hell. I mean, Riot is a very imposing man with his biker image and huge muscles. "You need to think about who the fuck you sleep with, man. He's one pansy-arse bitch who runs when his people need him."

"You can't say things like that. Ben, make him stop. We had something once. You can't let him speak to me like this." Harry has the audacity to look offended at what Riot is saying.

I scoff and look him in the eyes.

"We had *nothing*, thanks to you. I was all in, but you weren't." I know I've said the wrong thing when Harry's eyes go dark and his lips thin. But what has my stomach in knots is realising my lie.

I was never all in with him because of the man standing next to me.

"Oh, that's a joke. You were never in all the way, Ben. You were always fawning over this dumb knob, bitching about all the men he was shagging. Calling out his name in your sleep," Harry snaps

Fuck, I forgot about that. A few times, when I got drunk at the start of our relationship, I would bitch about seeing Riot with other men. I would tell him all the things I loved about him and ask why he wouldn't fuck me. I also talk in my sleep, big time. One time I was told by a friend that I quoted an entire conversation of a movie I love.

Fun times. Or maybe not, if you ask Harry.

"Aww, babe, did you dream of me?" Riot jokes, making me look at him. His smile is wide giving me a view of his white teeth, and he winks, telling me to play along.

"Can you blame me?" I join in.

"I dream of you too, baby. Oh fuck, I love that thing you do with your tongue." He stops talking and looks at Harry. "Did he do that thing with his tongue to you? Fuck me, he has me coming so hard and fast, I see stars, and do not get me started on the way he fucks my arse. Damn, he pounds the shit out of me. Swivels his hips. Shit, now I'm hard. Baby, I think we should get home."

We shouldn't talk about hard cocks right now. I'm solid in my jeans, and we're in a bloody supermarket. Nice job, Riot.

"That's disgusting—talking about your sex life in public," Harry hisses in disgust, his face taking on a look like he sucked on a lemon.

"That's because your sex life with Ben was fucking crap, fuckface." Riot's tone takes on a deep, serious sound. One that says, *don't fuck with me.*

He turns to the Harry, looking him square in the eyes. "Ben knows how to fuck, believe me. He also knows how to be loving, loyal and respectful, something you don't have. Not a fucking ounce. Did you know that he left Ben when he was beating beaten up by three guys who hated gays? Ran away like the pussy he is. Fucking coward."

His eyes are wide with shock at Riot's words, then turn angry as he looks at Harry, who has now taken on a sheepish look.

"You told me that Ben cheated on you with this man. You never mentioned that he got beaten up. I should have known something was wrong when one of your friends asked about Ben, and you got angry and cut off the conversation."

He takes a step back from Harry, then looks at me with sadness in his eyes.

"He lied to me about you—hell, to everyone. He's told anyone who will listen that you cheated on him and he broke up with you."

"Ever the dramatic Harry," I reply to him, and he nods.

"I'm sorry about what happened. I'll be sure to clear a few things up." He looks between Riot and me with a small smile on his face. "If this is real, I hope you're both happy."

"Oh, it's real," Riot grinds out, clearly still pissed at Harry. The now ex-boyfriend nods and leaves without another word to anyone.

116

We stand there for a few seconds, letting what the hell just happened sink in, and Riot's hand tightens on my hip.

Turning to look at him, I have the urge to lean in and kiss his jaw, to feel his stubble against my lips. It's something I've wished to do for so bloody long, in real life and my dreams. To be able to touch him whenever I want, to kiss him whenever I want feels, right. Then it hits me: I can do that.

Leaning in, I kiss his jaw, pressing my lips to the stubble there, loving the feel of the bristles against my sensitive skin. He sighs, his body losing some of the tension he's been carrying since he found me in this messed up situation.

"How did you know I was here?" I whisper so only he can hear me.

He grins. "Tracked you." My mouth pops open, but I quickly shut it.

"Damn, babe," he mutters, then drags his gaze from mine to glare at Harry. I swear, if looks could kill, Harry would be sliced and diced and scattered in the river Thames.

"You lost the best fucking thing you ever had, but your loss is my gain, motherfucker. Stay the hell away from my man, or your parents will need dental records to identify your body." With that, Riot uses his free hand to push the trolley away from my ex.

Without a backward glance, we finish up getting the items on my list, Riot adding his own. The sight of seeing him add foods and other items to mine, to keep at my house gives me the warm and fuzzies.

"You got everything?" he asks me, pulling me from my thoughts. I nod and we make our way to the till.

Once we've paid for our things, we walk to my car. No words are spoken as we load the bags inside. My lips still tingle from the kiss, my heart is still pounding in my chest and my dick is still hard, begging to be released from the prison of my jeans.

He wants some action, and I can't say I blame him especially when Riot bends over to place the bags into the boot of my car.

Denim hugs his arse, framing it for all to admire, but only I get to touch—well, I had better be. From his words and actions, I believe he'll be faithful to me.

"I'll follow you back to your home, yeah?" comes his gruff voice, pulling me from my eye-fucking.

Bringing my gaze up to meet his, I see he's smirking at me, after catching me staring at his arse.

"Yeah, okay," is all I say, and get into my car.

Sixteen

Riot

I sit on a stool in the kitchen and watch Ben put the food shopping away. The sense of being domestic hits me square in the chest. This is something I've never had nor ever wanted, until my feelings for Ben grew.

I may be a cunt of a biker, who deals in guns, drugs, and money, but I still feel. I am still human and know love, loyalty, and respect.

Watching my brothers find their old ladies made me look at my life and see it flit away. I will always live and bleed for the club, but wanting to share my day with someone when I get home means something to me. Whether I sound like a chick or not, I don't give a fuck. Everyone, even a dirty biker, deserves happiness.

I've seen Mayhem, Chaos, and Psycho share their shit with their women; the ups and downs. Nothing could pull those fuckers away from the women in their lives, and I want that. Fuck, I am having that.

"Riot," Ben calls. I blink and look at him to see him leaning against the counter, looking at me. "You, okay?"

Clearing my throat, I smile at him and nod. "Yeah, I'm good. You all done?" I ask pointing to the now empty bags.

"Yeah. You want a drink or something?"

"Or something," I state, getting to my feet. He watches me as I close the gap between us. His eyes widen and darken with lust, and I grin, knowing I have him and I haven't even touched him yet.

But I will soon.

Moving my feet so they are on the outside of his, my hands meet his waist. My whole-body buzzes from the closeness of our bodies, and I want to shift even closer. The images of us fucking relentlessly flash in my head, in all fucking positions possible, while he wears my patch on his back. Leather and ink.

I want to grip his hair, bite his neck, and suck on the skin. To mark him as mine. To hear him call out my name as I fuck him until he comes all over me, while he grips my biceps, hanging on for dear life.

Fuck, my cock goes into hyperdrive, as I press in closer, feeling his erection.

"I need to fuck you," is all I say.

"Then do it." His voice is deep, gravelly.

Fuck me. I want all of him, every inch. I want to suck him dry, have him suck me dry. Just the thought of him falling apart because of me makes me leak. I'm needy and hard for him. I want to be the one who rips him apart, only to stitch him back together, and him me.

"Fuck." I take his hand in mine, dragging him from the kitchen and into the living room, where I know he has a chair that stands out from the rest of his furniture. It has character, which is why he loves it.

Also, it is the prefect height for me to fuck him over.

Pulling him to me, I kiss him like our lives depend on it. As I fuck his mouth with my tongue, I unbuckle his belt, then open his jeans, before pushing them to the floor. Breaking the kiss, I reach for the hem of his t-shirt and rip it from his body.

When he brings his lips back to mine, our kiss becomes frenzied, and it's sexy as fuck. His hands land on my chest, sliding up slowly, removing my cut from my body, I watch as he carefully folds it and places it on the coffee table, before turning back to me.

The love and pride I feel for this man fucking blows into orbit.

I grip the back of my own t-shirt and pull it over my head, dropping it to the floor as Ben removes his boots and socks, then kicks his jeans the rest of the way off. Then he drops to his knees. His hands go to my belt, and once that's undone, he pulls the zipper down, and pops open the button.

"Fuck, you're big," he mutters as he pulls my cock out of its confines.

I push my jeans down over my hips, giving him better access. He leans in, buries his nose in my pubic hair, and inhales. Fuck me, I like that.

"Put me in your mouth, baby," I command, and thank the road gods, he listens.

Opening his mouth, he pokes his tongue out and licks me from base to tip. I watch as his lips encase the head of my cock, and then he sucks. A tremor of ecstasy rushes through my body, and my nipples harden. Bringing my hands up, I rub my thumbs over my nipples while I watch my cock slide into his mouth.

"Fuck, that's sexy," I grind out. My voice is deep as fuck, thick with the emotion this man is evoking in me. I flex my hips, pushing my cock deeper into his mouth.

His eyes lock on mine, desire swirling in them. He loves sucking my big, fat cock. Not that I blame him. It's a nice dick.

In and out, my shaft moves between his lips, his saliva coating very inch of me. I'm a big bloke, and most guys can't take my whole length, but it seems Ben can not only swallow all of me, but he really fucking enjoys doing it. It's hot as shit.

My hands reach for his head, holding him still while I fuck his mouth, but Ben doesn't let me take full control. He slides one of his hands between my arse cheeks, putting pressure on the taint, then my arsehole. I suck in a breath.

"Fuck me, I'm going to come if you keep doing that, babe."

His eyes twinkle with mischief as he pushes a finger into my arse, just like I did to him not long ago. My balls start to draw up, but I'm not ready to blow my load yet.

"Baby," I warn. He pulls my cock out of his mouth and sits back on his haunches.

"What?" he asks, grinning at me.

"Get the fuck on the chair. Arse in the air." He smiles at me, getting to his feet.

Needing to taste myself on him, I grip the back of his neck and slam his mouth onto mine. I can taste my cum on his lips. He moans, making my cock twitch.

Ben pulls back, turns on his heels, and steps over to the chair. I stand stock still, breathing heavily. My cock pulses as my man settles on the chair, placing one knee on the arm, the other on the seat. He grips the back, presenting his delicious arse to me.

He's completely bare, no hair in sight, just smooth, flawless skin. Holy fucking cocks in hell.

Ben looks over his shoulder at me with a smirk in place. He licks his lips as his eyes roam over my naked form. I wrap my palm around my cock, tugging up and down.

"Get me ready for you, Riot."

"Leo," I growl. "I want you to call out my name as I fuck you hard, baby."

"Eat me, Leo. Get my arse ready to take your thick cock."

"Fuck," I mutter.

I stalk forward and drop to my knees behind him, gripping his arse cheeks with my hands, parting them to bare his tight hole to me. After dropping some saliva down onto

122

his hole, I dive in with my tongue. I lap at his hole, getting it nice and wet, soft, and relaxed, ready to take me whole.

"Oh, shit," he groans.

The sound goes straight to my cock, making it leak all over floor.

With his cheeks parted, I keep licking, sucking, and nipping at his skin. His body is tight with need, but his hole is loosening up as I stretch it out, making it slack. I replace my tongue with my thumb and drag it over the area, loving the way it contracts at my touch.

"Fucking sexy," I say, then bite my lip.

"I need you in me, Leo. Please." The pleading in his voice sends shockwaves through me. I have had men beg me to shag them before, but hearing Ben do it does something else to me entirely.

I push my thumb into his arse, past the tight ring of muscle, and he hisses. But his body relaxes and accepts my digit. I move it in and out to relax him more, to prepare him to take my cock.

"More," he mutters.

Looking up at him, I see his eyes are closed while he bites down on the back of the vintage chair. The sweet look of desire on his face drives me on.

"Lube," I state.

"Top draw. Key's in the plant pot." Ben points to a small cabinet that has three draws.

I'm not sure how I feel about him having lube and most probably condoms in a cabinet in his living room, so I ask him about it.

"Why do you have these in here?" I find the key and open the lock, then pull the drawer open, and sure enough there are a few bottles of lube—different flavours going by the colours—and two boxes of condoms.

Looking over his shoulder at me, he grins.

"Jealous?" he asks. Shaking my head at him, I pick up a sealed bottle and an unopened box of condoms.

I love that he sits there waiting for me, not bothering to rush me. He wants this just as much as I do. Once I've opened both the bottle and condom box, I rip a foil packet open and slide the rubber down my dick.

Walking back over to my man, I watch as his eyes dilate with each step I take. The anticipation is building in both of us. This right here has been a fucking long time coming.

Moving in behind him, I pop open the lube and drop some onto my hand, then cover my shaft. I add more lube to my fingers, then coat his arsehole, pushing some inside, making sure he's primed and ready to take me.

With my cock lined up, I nudge his arse. I kiss his back, then his neck, and his body buzzes beneath my touch. Goosebumps cover his skin, along with a thin layer of sweat.

"Ben, I'll stop when you ask me to. I will never take from you, only give you what you want. I want to feel you, taste you. I want to touch you, always. You give this delectable arse to me, and I'll be yours, and you will be mine, babe."

"Fucking hell, Leo. You can't say shit like that to me when you're about to fuck me. I am yours, and you're mine. Like I said before, I write thriller, crime, and mystery books. I know how to get rid of a body. So fuck me already and finish the claim," Ben pants out, sticking his arse out, offering himself to me.

And damn am I hungry.

Putting my knee next to his, I hold my dick tighter, then start to push in. The tightness of him grips my cock, and we moan as I push in further. Once the head breaks through, Ben hisses at the sensation, and I growl.

"Holy fuck, you feel good. So damned tight."

I hold still for what feels like ages, then Ben relaxes, arching his back a little more. Moving a hand to his thigh, my other hand grips the top of the chair as I start to move in and out of him, the lube helping me to slide in effortlessly.

I grind my hips down, going deeper and deeper, as Ben growls and groans in ecstasy. As I tighten my grip on the chair, he pants out my name, making me want to ram him hard, but I don't—well, not yet.

Moving my leg, I put my foot back onto the floor, gripping his hips firmly, and start to move faster. We breathe heavier between groans and growls. I bring a hand up and slap it back down on his arse cheek, loving it when I see the skin turn pink from the spanking.

"Yeah, baby." I do it again.

Ben groans and pushes back against me, wanting more. He moves further down the chair, giving me more of his arse, and I pound in and out of him, enjoying the feel of his tightness around my cock. He's strangling me, begging for me to make him come.

"Fuck, I feel so fucking full," Ben groans.

"Fuck yeah, you do. My big, fat cock is in your tight arse. Best arse I've ever fucked," I reply, picking up the pace.

My hand finds the back of his neck holding him in place—not that he's going anywhere. Bending forward, I kiss between his shoulder blades, then his neck.

Without warning, I pull out, then turn him around and drag him up so I can kiss his beautiful mouth.

"Back on the chair, on your back. I want to see your face when we come," I state.

Ben smiles at me and kisses me quickly before he turns and sits his arse down on the chair, then adjusts himself so his arse is hanging over the edge, his legs in the air.

"You love offering your arse up to me, don't you, baby?" I grin down at him.

"Only you, Leo."

"Fuck yeah, only me."

I line my cock up with his arse and push back in. This time, his hole accepts me greedily, like it's made for me.

"Oh fuck," he pants out, taking me in deeper. Heaven surrounds my cock as I breathe in heavy, relishing in the sensation.

Seventeen

Ben

My body tenses from the intrusion of Riot's thick dick in my arse. My eyes are wide, I know it, and my mouth open in ecstasy. Leo looks down at me with dark eyes, showing his arousal.

He has never let anyone call him Leo, not since his shitty parents. When he joined the club, he was always causing some kind of riot, so the name was given to him, and it stuck.

My hands jump to his biceps, holding on as he slowly moves in and out of me, stretching my arse inch by inch. The burn feels good; it makes my dick jerk and leak over my abs.

The way he grips the back of my thighs keeps me open for him, and he looks down, watching his cock slide in and out of me.

I watch his face as he focuses on his cock disappearing into me. Sweat covers him, droplets gliding down his skin, into the light sprinkling of hair that covers his chest.

"Oh, fuck," I growl when he bottoms out, hitting my prostate.

My balls go tighter than a nun's vagina, begging for release. We pant together, breathing in the sex-filled air. Leo brings his eyes to mine, and we become locked in a sex-induced gaze.

127

"Fuck me, you are beautiful," he grinds out, his teeth clenching as his hips slap against my arse.

His words hit me in the balls, and they go incredibly tighter. Leo has been with so many men, so him saying that to me means a lot.

Smiling at him, I bring my hand to his cheek, rubbing my thumb over his stubble. I gasp as he slams against me, sending his cock surging deep. He holds his position, neither of us moving as we let this moment sink in.

His cock pulses inside of me but I know he hasn't come. It's just the nerves firing off before the final explosion.

Only the sounds of our heavy breathing can be heard in the room, but I can smell the sex around us. It's a potent fragrance. If I could bottle it and sell it, I would make a mint.

Leo licks his lips before moving in to kiss me, and my legs drop to wrap around his waist. His mouth devours mine and his tongue tangles with my own, dominating the kiss from the get-go—not that I'm complaining about that. He can do whatever the hell he wants to me.

I mean, have you seen him?

My hands are on the back of his neck, holding him to me. Not that he would leave right now; his dick is in prime position.

"Do you know how long I've wanted to have you? To be buried deep inside you? Fuck, Ben," he grinds out after breaking the kiss.

His forehead rests against mine as he moves slowly, dragging his cock out, stilling, then sliding back in. I hiss as pleasure lances through my body. We stare at each other, getting lost in the fire burning between us.

With each thrust of his hips, I can feel my orgasm building. Sometimes, if the sex is good, I don't need to touch my dick, just like right now, but I want to come hard for my first time with Riot, so I reach down between us and grip my cock, which is pulsing with so much need it's vibrating.

"Oh, fuck. That's some hot shit. Make yourself come, baby. I'm almost there." Riot growls, watching me wank off as he fucks my arse. "Yes. Come!" he bellows.

At his demand, I come all over my stomach, hot white streams hitting my skin. I hold my breath, something I do when I climax as it heightens the orgasm. Leo chases his own, slamming his hips against my arse until he growls fiercely, a sound I have never heard from him before.

It's deep and gravelly, tortured even, as he fills me up.

His body goes weak as he falls against me, and my arms instinctively wrap around his back, holding him to me while we both catch our breaths. He has a small smattering of hair on his back, so I trace my fingers through it.

Dipping my head forward, I kiss his bare shoulder, breathing in his heady scent, as I taste him on my lips.

This here, right now, feels nice, feels right. For years I have wanted what we just did and more, and I feel like I'm dreaming.

Am I dreaming? It would be shitty if I am.

"You're not dreaming, Ben." His deep voice vibrates through my body, making my dick twitch.

Shit, again? Really?

This is what this man does to me.

"Shit, did I say that out loud?" I ask him.

Leo lifts his head to bring his gaze to mine. He gives me a dreamy smile, leaning in to kiss me. Slowly, he backs his hips away, pulling his softening dick from my sore, aching arse, making me wince.

"Does that feel like a dream? Did the hard fucking and hard orgasm feel like a dream?"

Grinning at him. "No, it felt fucking amazing." I go to say more but Riot's stomach grumbles, making us both laugh.

He gets to his feet, standing unashamed in front of me with a full condom hanging from his dick, which still looks huge, even though he is soft.

"You keep looking at my cock like that and round two will come around a lot quicker than you think, babe," he growls.

"Come on, let me make you something. I could eat too," I tell him and get to my feet.

Before I've got my balance, Riot is pulling me to him, gripping my jaw with one hand, the other going to my arse cheek. Then he's taking my mouth in a kiss that leaves no room for doubt as to who I belong to, nor who he belongs to.

The kiss is slow, sensual, and full of meaning.

He takes my breath away with how sweet and gentle he can be, while most think he's a scummy, criminal biker. Don't get me wrong, he is a criminal, but aren't most people? Don't most people break the law in one way, shape or form?

When I pull back, he keeps his eyes on me. A smile graces his sexy mouth, and he kisses me once more before he steps around me.

"Let's go and make something to eat. I need to keep you well fed if I'm going to take a few more times tonight."

His words shock me but also excite me, and my hardening dick approves. Once in the kitchen, I open the fridge and start pulling out the fixings to make him a chicken and vegetable stir fry, which I know he loves.

In a flash, I'm bent over at the waist. My chest hits the cold worktop and I hiss, but then a warm, soothing feeling hits my arse. Looking over my shoulder I see Riot on his knees, cleaning me up, making sure he gets all the lube he used.

I breathe slowly, loving the feel of the warm cloth, and my heart swells at the thought of him taking care of me. Like he can hear my thoughts, he stands up, and I see the cloth go flying towards the bin.

"I'll always take care of you, Ben Miller. Always, baby. You're mine now." He taps my bum cheek and takes a seat at the island to watch me cook.

I rustle up a chicken stir fry, adding the ingredients. This is one of my favourite meals to make—well, this and a good old-fashioned Sunday roast. If you ask Logan, I make the best mac and cheese with sausage ever, so that's a win in my book.

Anything that makes my nephew smile is a win.

Once the food is cooked, I add some to two bowls and place one in front of Riot, before taking a seat across from him. He cocks an eyebrow at me with a challenging look.

"What?" I ask him. He looks from me to the stool next to him, then back to me.

Oh, he wants me to sit next to him. Right.

I push my bowl across the island and walk around to him. My arse hits the smooth but cold seat and I shiver, making Riot grin at me.

"Prick," I mutter. He leans in and kisses my bare shoulder, before tucking into his food.

He moans and hums in appreciation, making my dick twitch and jerk with need for him. The way his lips wrap around the fork is a bloody turn on. Can someone be jealous of an inanimate object? A fucking fork at that.

Licking my lips, I force my gaze away and eat my food before it gets cold.

"Fuck, this is good, babe." He moans again. I swear he's doing that on purpose.

Riot likes to eat. Hell, he has to if he wants to keep his body in the shape it is. He needs to eat more calories than me because he's bigger, plus he does more than me. While I finish off the bowl, I watch as Riot gets up and moves around my kitchen like he belongs there, helping himself to seconds, and I get a pang in my heart at the sight.

I abandon my food when my stomach tightens with need—as well as my balls. My cock is begging to be played with at the sight of a very naked Leo walking around like he lives here.

Fuck, the thought of Riot and me living together sets my heart racing. My eyes widen at the thought of him being here all the time, coming home to me after working at the garage, or after a run. Him looking after me when I'm on a deadline.

Holy crap.

This is fucking fast—way too bloody fast to be thinking like this, surely.

"Hey, you okay?" His voice breaks through my panic attack, and my wide eyes focus on him.

He frowns, looking me over, trying to find a problem. I swallow hard, licking my dry lips before I answer him.

"Yeah. Just seeing you be free and content walking around naked in my home got me horny again," I lie, but Riot sees through it.

"Ben, you will always be horny when I'm around. I know I'm a fucking hot bloke." He winks at me, and I laugh. "But do not lie to me. What freaked you out?"

Sighing, I turn in my seat a little to face him better.

"It's nothing," I tell him, making sure to look him in the eye.

"Ben, baby, stop this shit and tell me. I can see in your eyes that you thought of something that freaked you out. Have I not shown you that I only want you?"

Fucking hell, I know he won't let this lie.

"Seeing you walking around got stupid images in my head of us living together, okay. I know it's stupid, and way too fucking soon. I mean, we only just had sex for the first time." I huff, then get off my seat and take my bowl over to the sink.

I dump the now cold food into the food recycling bin, then place my bowl in the sink. Resting my palms on the side,

I hang my head, trying to breathe slowly and push the images out of my head. I know it's way too fucking soon, but it feels right thinking it. Riot is behind me, not moving, so I know I've freaked him out too. I'm waiting for him to bolt, because he was never one to commit this much this soon. Never one to commit to anything.

Shit, I just ruined everything before it even got off the ground.

Nice one, Benny boy.

Heat at my back has my spine straightening. Riot's hands settle on my waist and his lips skim my shoulder, making me shiver. My nipples peak, and my dick takes note of the touch.

Nothing is said right away. We just stand there, naked as the day we were born, touching from thighs to head. The feel of his skin against mine is heavenly; hot, smooth, and hard.

"Fuck," I mutter when I feel his teeth sinking into my shoulder as he thrusts his hips against my arse, pushing his hard dick into my flesh.

"Ben, I wanted you then, I want you now, and I will fucking want you fifty years from now. This arse is the best I've ever had."

"Just my arse?" I reply as his words wash over me. He pinches my side, making me jolt. "Prick."

He chuckles behind me, then kisses my shoulder again. "Face me," he commands into my ear.

I do as he says, and the movement causes my cock to brush against his. My body goes on alert from the contact, and my balls draw up with arousal for this man. He cups my face, making me look him in the eyes. Leaning in, he kisses me with open eyes then pulls away.

"Not just your arse. All of you, Ben. I may sound like a chick but fuck it. Men love and feel too. I may be a dirty biker, and I may be a criminal, but I can love just as much as the next guy. People will say it's too soon but fuck it. We've known each other for years, both felt the connection. It may

133

not have happened when we first wanted it to, but it's happening now. No fucker gets a say in this relationship except me and you. It's the Ben and Riot show, baby. Fuck everyone else.

"I've claimed you, Ben, in the eyes of the club. And one day soon, I'll brand you as mine, so everyone knows who you belong to. Who I belong to. You want me to move in, I'll move in. Hell, I stay at the clubhouse because I had no reason to buy a home, so I'm more than happy to move in with you, but only if you want that too."

I find myself nodding because I can't make my voice work. Riot grins a wicked smile at me making me shiver. What the fuck just happened? Did he just tell me he's moving in with me and I agreed? Holy fucking shit.

"Good. Now get on your fucking knees and suck my cock."

Sliding down the cupboard behind me, I balance on the balls of my feet, putting my face flush with his thick cock, which is leaking pre-cum.

I bring my hand up and grip him, before guiding the head to my mouth. I rub his pre-cum over my lips, and Riot growls, his eyes turning molten at the sight. Smirking up at him, I open my mouth, letting his cock stretch my lips. This is not the first time I've sucked him off, and fuck me, he feels as good in my mouth now as he did the first time.

"Fuck, yeah, Ben," he moans above me.

His hands rest on the counter behind me as he forces his cock to the back of my throat, my head hitting the unit behind me as he cages me in. With my head locked in place, Riot starts rutting his hips, effectively fucking my mouth, and I fucking love it.

I like all kinds of sex; nothing really turns me off.

The Riot I'm having right now is the harder Riot, the dirty biker Riot who likes to fuck hard and rough.

Keeping my eyes locked on him, watching him as he gets engulfed in the euphoria of this blowjob, I take in his ruggedly handsome face, my pride welling that it's me doing this to him. Bringing my hands up, I cup his balls and tug on them while my other hand finds my cock, and I wank myself off in time with Riot fucking my mouth.

"Stop. Your orgasms are mine," he growls, only making me hotter.

My hand drops from my dick, and in a flash, Riot is pulling his dick from my mouth and stepping back. He offers his hands to me and pulls me to my feet, then kisses me hard and long while we thrust, rubbing our dicks together.

"Over on the bench," he commands, and I listen.

I mean, who wouldn't listen to their man if they were as hot and sexy as Leo Peters? I walk over to the dining table, to the bench next to it, and turn to face the man.

"On your back," he tells me. I do as he commands, my legs hanging over either side.

Riot moves in to straddle the bench and pushes my legs up, before diving in with his tongue to get my hole ready to take him again. I wince because I'm a little sore, and Riot looks up at me.

"I'm good. Carry on," I beg.

"Oh, I know how good you are, baby," he replies and goes back to eating my hole.

I moan, growl and hiss at the feel of what he's doing. The feel of his short beard rubbing against my sensitive skin turns me on to no end. He adds a finger, then two, stretching me to take him.

"I'm ready, Leo. Fuck me already," I pant out.

Riot smirks at me, then moves in close to me, my legs still in the air as he lines his cock up then looks at me again. The heat I see in his eyes makes me leak all over my stomach.

135

"I want you raw, Ben. Will you let me?" His question shocks me, but again I find myself nodding. "I've never gone raw before. You're the first."

"Same here. Do it," I growl out.

The thought of Riot inside of me with nothing between us makes me pant with need for him. I watch as he drops spit down on my arse and his cock, getting them wet before he slides into me.

The pressure of his cock makes me hiss, and I fall back onto the bench. Inch by slow inch he moves into me, until he comes to a sop and pants from the sensation.

"Oh fuck, that feels like nothing I have ever felt before. Holy fuck I'm going to come quick as fuck, Ben. You need to come with me."

I grip the backs of my thighs, holding myself open for him while he moves in and out of me. He places two hand on the bench for leverage and starts fucking me fast and hard.

We pant and moan, growling each other's names.

He fucks me long and deep for a time, never once pulling his cock from my tight arse. With his feet planted on the floor, he shifts so he is on top of me, fucking me hard and fast again.

"So much for coming quick. It seems to make you go longer, harder. Fuck yes," I growl.

The sound of our skin slapping together fills my kitchen, his balls hitting my own with force. My own balls start to tighten ready to explode all over us. In a flash, he adjusts our bodies, he's lying on his back, dragging me over his body, then I'm riding his cock. Deep and hard.

My hand goes to his throat, holding on, while his go behind his head, as he watches me fuck him. I take my dick in hand, jerking in time with my bouncing on his shaft.

Riot drops his gaze from mine, watching where we are connected. I watch as his eyes darken, and knowing it's because of me, I come.

He grips my hips, watching my face as I come all over his abs. My heart is racing like a speed train, but I hear his voice.

"Lift up." With my feet planted on the floor, I lift off his cock, and he comes with a growl over his abs, his seed mixing with mine.

I bend forward, running my tongue through the white liquid, tasting us together.

"Holy shit, that's hot," he says from above me. "Share." I smile and scoop up some of our cum with my tongue, then move to kiss him, letting the liquid slide into his mouth.

We kiss and moan as our mixed essence is tasted by us both. My dick jerks at the action wanting to go again. Lying here naked, covered in sweat and cum, and kissing Riot is like a dream. I can only hope and fucking pray that nothing breaks us.

I know his past, I know his history, but I also know how loyal he is, so I just have to hope that his loyalty to me sticks and is enough to keep him from straying.

Eighteen

Riot

Another run has taken me away from Ben. After the weekend we just had, I didn't want to leave him, but this new run is a big fucker. This is our biggest shipment yet. It's with a new crew that was put in contact with us by one of our other clients, so they should be safe. But we know how things can hit the fan. I hate not knowing who we are working with, but Chaos and Psycho checked them out, so we are good to go.

Today we are in the larger van, pulling a trailer with a fucking speed boat on it, carrying a tonne of drugs, and guns. Plus, we have three cars and two bikes. Working on these took a while, but as a club we got it done in time. Getting this amount of product was easy with our contacts in London and other parts of England, plus my chick in Wales. Miss I is one woman you do not want to cross when it comes to her deals.

Pulling into a different location, I see a white Ranger Rover parked close to an expensive-looking sports car. I park the van, the boys pulling in one by one with the other items we are handing over, and pray this goes to plan because I want to get home to my man and get some dicking done before he goes to bed.

He's worked his arse off editing and proofing his latest book and has been tired the last few nights. Plus, I rammed his arse pretty hard over the weekend and he needed the break, but now I'm in need of some tight arse loving.

I switch the van off and climb out, walking over to the posh cars with my brothers at my side. Chaos shakes the suit's hand, while my gaze scans over the other men he has with him, all in similar monkey suits.

Words are exchanged, so are keys, and then the money, which is the part that makes me smile. We always deal in cold hard cash; it's easier to hide. Mayhem hands over the four large black duffle bags to two prospects, and then walks them over to the van that carries our bikes.

My body feels tight tonight, edgy even, but nothing is coming to mind as to why I feel like this. I know it has nothing to do with Ben, because I'll see him soon, the drop here seems to be going okay, and I don't get a bad vibe from the buyers.

I shake it off and keep my wits about me while the deal is winding down.

"Nice doing business with you, Wreckers. I'll see how these sell, and if my clients are happy, I will be in touch." With that, the man gets into his sports car and bombs it off down the road, followed by the Ranger Rover and the vehicles we dropped off. Damn, I'm going to miss that boat.

"Brothers, it's time to celebrate. That was our biggest sell to date, and we are fucking rolling in the paper." Chaos beams. "Clubhouse, drinks, then pussy," he calls as we walk over to our bikes.

"Fuck yeah," goes around, everyone smiling. Then something pops into my head.

"Fuck, I have to do a pickup," I shout to them. "I forgot that Rob is late on his payment. I need to shake that prick up. I'll catch up with you."

They nod and pull out of the small parking lot.

139

I take my time on the road because we had some rain today and the tarmac looks slick. I don't fancy skidding and removing the skin from my body. Road rash hurts like a bitch.

It doesn't take me long to hit the street where Rob's little dive kebab shop is. The fucker should be shut down, but he always manages to get away with it. He must be buying people off.

When I park my bike, I shut her down and climb off, before removing my helmet and setting it on my seat. The lights are off in the front, but I see a light on in the kitchen. I bang on the window but get nothing, so I bang again. I see shadows moving, so I know someone is in there.

"Fucking prick. You're keeping me from fucking my man tonight and drinking with my brothers," I grumble as I walk around the back, to get in through the kitchen.

I reach the back door and bang on that. Shuffling sounds come from the other side, and now I'm pissed.

"Open the fuck up, Rob. You owe the club money, and you're keeping me away from my man. You do not want to get on my bad side when I want my man."

More shuffling comes, and my anger spikes. No fucker steals from the Road Wreckers MC and that's what this cunt is doing by not paying, so now I need to make him pay up with a little beat down. That also sends a message to all the other scummy fucks who borrow money from us—that you can't withhold the payments, otherwise we come knocking twice has hard.

With a clenched fist, I bang the door for the last time, before I begin to force my way in.

"Open up. Last chance," I yell.

"Fuck, wait! Wait. I'm opening the door." Rob says, his voice shaky. His tone makes me go on high alert, and for good reason.

My anger is already at boiling point, but when Rob pulls the door open and I see a little punk right behind him aiming a gun at me, I fucking explode. I charge forward, knocking them both to the ground, but not before the fucker fires.

"Die, faggot," I hear him scream.

A searing pain goes through my shoulder, and it fuels my anger. Scrambling over Rob, I grab the little fuck by the neck of his jumper and bring my fist back to hit him, over and over again. My fist connects with his jaw, cheekbones, and nose. Bones crunch, but I don't stop. The cunt shot me.

All I see is red, as images of Ben flash in my mind at thoughts of the bullet hitting me in the chest or neck. I would never see him again, hold him, kiss him.

"Fucking cunt," I bellow at the man.

I'm breathing heavily, and my arm starts to lose its momentum. The blood loss is taking its toll. Fuck. The prick manages to get a few hits against my ribs and stomach, but that doesn't stop me. I don't think anything will stop me from killing him.

Looking down at the man, I see his face is barely recognisable. Blood covers it, coating my knuckles.

"Riot, man, you need to stop, or you will kill him." Rob's voice is just as shaky as it was when he opened the door, but now his fear is clear as day.

Pushing off the half dead man, I get to my feet, looking down at him, breathing like I just ran a 10k run. Sweat covers my body, making my t-shirt cling to me. I spy the gun a few feet away, so I step over to pick it up.

"Anyone else here?" I ask him. Rob shakes his head. "Call Chaos," I tell Rob, as my body sways and my knees give out.

The balding man catches me and helps me to the floor, before pulling his phone out and doing as I said. I faintly hear him talking to Prez before everything goes black.

Nineteen

Ben

I pour hot water into my Marvel mug and stir the spoon around, before adding milk and sweeteners. I need a nice cup of tea to relax after another day of editing, readying my manuscript to go to my professional editor, who makes my books more readable. She is one crazy chick; she makes me laugh with her comments and isn't afraid to tell me if a scene is shit or not.

Friday whines from her position by the door, letting me know she wants to go outside to relieve herself. I walk over and pull the door open before she bolts down to her tree. My phone rings from the kitchen island, but it rings off before I can get to it. Picking up the device, I see it's my brother calling me.

Before I can call him back, it rings again, and something tells me that something has happened, and it's bad. My stomach clenches as I answer.

"Scott?"

"Thank fuck. You need to get to the clubhouse; Riot has been hurt." His voice is strained so I know it's bad.

My stomach sinks into the tiled floor beneath my bare feet at hearing my boyfriend has been hurt. How? When? Where? How bad is it?

"What happened?" I ask, my voice shaking. Fear taking over.

"Just get here, Benny. I'll explain then. Mum and Dad are on their way." Then he ends the call.

I rush over to the back door and call Friday to come.

Then I franticly run around the house and get dressed, pulling on my trainers and grabbing a few things I will need because I'm not leaving my man while he heals. He didn't leave me when I was healing, and we weren't even together.

"Come on, girl, Riot is hurt." Friday whines but follows me out to my car.

I help her in, then snap in her seatbelt, throw my bag in, and jump inside. On the drive to the clubhouse, all sorts of messed up things rush through my head, mixing with an abundance of horror movie scenes.

Was he jumped like me? Did he get shot? Did a car fall on him in the garage?

Bloody hell, never in my life did I think something like this would happen to Riot. He's always seemed invincible to me. I have seen the members of the club get cuts and scrapes but never something serious. Fuck, I've helped clean a few up in my time, but this time, my heart knows it's worse.

I stall my car at the traffic lights, my body not co-operating as is shakes with adrenaline and worry for my man.

Never in a million years did I think I would be calling Riot, aka Leo Peters, my man, and there is no way in another million that I'll lose him now. I may not be a tough guy, but I will hunt down anyone who hurts him, and I'll make them pay.

When I pull up to the front gates, the prospect opens them for me, giving me a grim look as I pass. My anxicty skyrockets at that look. Oh my God, is Riot dead?

I park my car and quickly knock off the engine, then climb out and run into the clubhouse. Pushing through the

143

door, I stop in my tracks when I see everyone mulling around. There is a sad air tainting the atmosphere.

"Where is he?" I call to the room.

Psycho steps over to me, giving me a look that tells me to get my shit together before I blow a gasket, but I will explode unless someone starts talking.

"Where is he?" I snap.

Psycho cocks an eyebrow at me, surprised that I took that tone with him. Fuck, so am I, but right now I need information on Riot and he's just standing there looking like a fucking silent biker Devil ninja.

"He's in with the doc. He's alive right now."

"What happened? And do not give me that club business bullshit," I grind out. The corner of his mouth turns up a fraction, and he crosses his arms over his chest.

"It is club business," he replies, and my anger takes over my anxiety. I step forward and he grins devilishly, but it doesn't stop me. However, an arm on my bicep does.

Turning my head, I see my brother standing there looking downright pissed, but I can see the worry in his eyes. His gaze bounces from me to Psycho, then back to me, assessing the situation.

"It is club business, Benny. All I can say is that he was on a collection and shit got out of hand. The guy he was collecting from was being robbed, and Riot interrupted it. He took a bullet to the shoulder. The doc is in there now, pulling the bullet out. He lost a good amount of blood and is weak as fuck right now. You can go and see him, when—"

I don't let him finish. I run past him and down the hall to the medical room. Pushing the door open, I see the doc bending over Riot, cleaning up his shoulder. My eyes drift to my man, seeing he's lying flat on his back, shirtless, eyes closed. I lower my gaze to watch his chest rise and fall. It's only then that my body relaxes some. There's some small bruising on his ribs, maybe from a fight. Did he fight back?

"Ben," Riot says, pulling my observation from his chest.

"I'm here. Fuck, you scared me," I tell him, looking down at him.

He gives me a weak smile, his head lulling to the side. I look at the doc in a panic, but he gives me a reassuring smile.

"He's fine. It's the blood loss and the drugs I've given him. The bullet lodged between the bone and muscles but I got it out. From what I can see there is no damage, and he should be fine in a day or two, but he needs to take it easy with the shoulder. He was lucky." I nod at his words and look down at Riot again.

I watch as the doc finishes up with Riot's shoulder. When he's done, he goes to leave but stops by the door and talks to Chaos and Mayhem. He explains to them what he has done and how things will be with Riot. I listen to them, but keep my gaze on Riot, my hands tightly wrapped around one of his.

My gaze moves over his body, checking for other injuries. Even though I know the doc said he is fine, I need to check for myself, so my heart can go back to its normal rhythm. Seeing the blood on his bicep and at the corner of his mouth, I look around the room to find what I need to clean him up.

While I'm cleaning the blood off his face, my brother and Chaos come into the room.

"Doc said he will be fine in a day or two. Lucky fucker," Scott pipes up, and I snap.

"Lucky? Are you fucking serious? He could have been killed. Why the hell was he doing a collection on his own? You never do this shit solo."

"Watch it, Ben. You may be Mayhem's brother and Riot's old man, but you fucking remember who you're speaking to," Chaos snarls at me.

Fucking hell. I reel in my attitude for now. Pissing off the president of the club is not something I want to do. But how could they let him go alone? He told me not long ago that they never do collections alone. They always go in pairs.

"He wanted to pop in for the collection on the way to you. Rob is harmless. Riot didn't know he was being fucking robbed," Mayhem tells me. I shake my head and stand to my full height, looking at Chaos and my brother.

"That doesn't mean shit right now and you know it. You all say you're there for each other, but tonight you weren't there for him. He could have been killed tonight. I could have lost the man I love, because you guys wanted to get your dicks wet rather than back up one of your own."

"BEN." Riot's bellowing voice fills the room, making me stop my ranting. "Enough."

I look down at him and watch in shock and anger as he forces himself to sit up. I go to help but he growls at me. My heart hurts at the look in his eyes, at the anger he has for me. Anger I put it there.

My body goes solid and cold at the icy look he's giving me.

"You will never speak to my president like that again, do you hear me? It was my choice to do the collection alone, not theirs. No fucker will tell me what to do, and you should know that. The men needed to get home and I went to visit Rob. He's a fucking weasel, but like Mayhem said, he's harmless. I'm a fucking adult. Not even you can tell me what the fuck to do. Just because we fuck, it doesn't mean you get to run my life for me."

"Brother," Mayhem warns, but Riot keeps going as I stand there, stock still, letting his words turn my blood to ice. Shaking his head, Riot continues.

"The club comes first, over everything. They are my fucking life, my blood, and I will do whatever is needed of me. No dick will change that. I thought you knew about club life but it seems I was fucking wrong," he grinds out.

My throat tightens, and my eyes fill with unshed tears.

Nodding, l look away from him and turn to my brother.
"Thanks for the call. I'm glad your brother is okay."
With that, I leave the room without looking back.
"Ben, wait," Scott calls to me, but I don't stop.

Rushing down the hall and into the main room, I ignore the calls from my parents and the stares from the other club members. Friday whines as she keeps pace with me, until we get to my car. After helping her in, I get behind the wheel and peel away from the clubhouse, wanting to be as far away from them and Riot as I can be right now.

Today is the last day I come here. He just ruined anything we ever had, and my heart is breaking piece by piece. Tears fall down my face as I head to my house. My plan is to lock myself away from the world and finish my damned book. That will take my mind off the excruciating pain in my chest.

Riot's words wash over me as I pull up to my house, park in the garage, then let Friday out. She runs through the open door that leads into the garden. Following her, I move down the side of the house and close the gate, locking the world out.

My phone vibrates in my pocket. Pulling it out, I see my brother is calling me. I ignore it and the call finally stops, but then it starts again. A text comes through from my mum, but I don't read it. I don't need to. I know it's her making sure I'm okay, or maybe threatening Riot.

Switching my phone off, I walk into my house, leaving the back door open for my baby to come in and out as she pleases. I pull a bottle of beer out of the fridge and finish it in one go, then reach for another. After the third bottle, I slow down and take the forth bottle into the living room. I kick off my trainers, remove my t-shirt, and throw myself down on the couch.

My tears have dried up but my heart is still breaking, however I know I'll survive this. Some see me as soft because I'm gay and write books for a living, but fuck me, I am strong when I need to be. I'm loyal, I love hard, and I'll give you the shirt off my back if you need it.

Picking up the TV remote, I flick through Netflix, trying to find some action shit where people die. I need something to take my mind off all the shit that's swirling around my head.

I see Riot's angry face—fuck me, he wasn't angry; he was enraged. He didn't see or care that I was hurting at seeing him hurt. He didn't see my fear of losing him. All he saw was me being disrespectful to his brothers, which means he doesn't know me at all, and now he never will.

If being with Harry has taught me anything, it's that I'm worthy of so much more than the way people treat me. Only my family respect me, and my self-respect is higher than it used to be. I'm proud to be me. Clearly, Riot was in this for the sex. He wanted to curb that craving he's had for me for years. It was all a motherfucking game.

And I'm done.

No more men.

I need to focus on my writing and enjoy single life; go and do things that don't involve other people.

Now, I'll live for me.

Twenty

Riot

MOTHINGFUCKING CUNT ON A STICK.

I fucked up. I know it. Everyone in the club knows it.

When I get on pain meds, it makes me an evil bastard. For some reason, I turn into a nasty piece of work; always have done. Some people turn into nasty drunks or pieces of shit on drugs. Me, I go all Lucifer when I take pain meds, which is why I try to never take any form of pain medicine if I can help it.

The doc should have warned Ben. Hell, my brothers should have warned him.

I could hear the fear in his voice, the anger directed at Prez over what happened. I wanted to comfort him, to tell him I was okay, but the ugly black fog took over and I snapped.

It was like I couldn't stop talking and ended up saying shit I didn't mean. I knew he meant well, and once the painkillers wore off and Mayhem told me what I said, I felt like the biggest cunt in the world.

Now it's four days later and Ben won't take my calls. He won't reply to my texts. Mayhem told me to give him time to cool off, so that's what I'm doing. I've thrown myself into ordering the prospects around, making them do my jobs around the garage for me, because my arm is still in a sling. Which is a bitch, by the way.

I'm like a bear with a sore head and I have the biggest case of blue balls I have ever had, knowing my man is hating on me. Everyone is keeping their distance. No doubt they are sick of me snapping at them. Shit, I'm a right old prick.

Fuck.

Twenty-One

Ben

My laptop screen goes black as it shuts down. I've done all my proofreading for the day, and the book is now ready to go to my editor. I've been at it for five days, throwing myself into my world. Not only have I finished proofing this one, but I started a new MC series, based in the UK.

I've read some amazing MC books over the years. One of my favourites is the Hawks MC by Lila Rose. That woman knows how to get the blood pumping and the juices flowing. Speaking of other authors, I'm meeting up with a few fellow writers soon to talk about a signing we're all attending. I love signings because I get to mingle with other authors and the amazing readers, who make me laugh.

It was this group of writers who convinced me to try my hand at MC romance. My series is plotted out, and I've found a few covers that are hot. I mean, who doesn't like a shirtless man with a body to die for, tattoos, and a beard?

Pushing back from the desk, I grab my phone from the wireless charger to text my brother.

Me: Is Logan ready for today?

I go into the kitchen to pack the small backpack I'm using for the day. I add in some snacks he loves and some fruit

151

drinks. Today, I'm taking Logan swimming. I need a change of pace. I need to push everything out of my head, and all my focus will be solely on my nephew if I spend the day with him.

Over the past few days, I've ignored Riot's calls and texts. I'm done. Nothing he can say will ever make up for the way he treated me. Even as I think that, my heart aches. He made me believe I meant something to him.

Scott: Yeah, but you need to pick him up at the club. I had to bring him with me this morning.

My heart clenches at the thought of going to the club. Even though I've spoken to Chaos and apologised, I've avoided the club, not wanting to see Riot or listen to his shitty excuses—not that he would give any. I meant nothing to him.

Me: Can you bring him to the gate?

Childish, I know, but I don't want to see him.

Scott: No.

No? That's all I get?

I don't bother replying because I know it's futile to argue with him. Stubborn dick. I finish up packing what I need and get Friday settled in the car.

The drive to the clubhouse is one filled with anxiety. I bite my nails, which is something I never do, between tapping my fingers on the steering wheel. Switching the radio on, it automatically connects to my phone and starts playing my playlist.

But the music doesn't soothe my nerves.

The prospect opens the gate when I arrive, sending my stomach into a knot sailors would be proud of.

I park my car and get out, then wait for Scott to bring Logan to me. I lean on the hood of my car, my gaze scanning the compound yard, and my heart sinks into my trainers. Sitting and watching the car wreck in front of me, I'm frozen in place.

Riot walks out of the garage, pulling his t-shirt over his head, then slides on his cut. The man he's talking to is smiling at him, and he's retuning it wider than normal. They seem like they have an intimate connection by the way they're standing next to each other.

My gaze is locked on them, my body feeling like cement. The man touches Riot's arm, and I expect him to brush him off, but he doesn't. He looks down at the hand, then smiles up at the man. My heart shatters as I watch the man lean in and kiss Riot. Again, I expect him to push him away, but for a few seconds, he kisses him back.

"UNCLE BEN," Logan calls.

Riot pulls away from the man, his head snapping in my direction. I see the shock on his face, then a scowl forms, but I look away, not wanting to see any more.

"Hey, bud. You ready?" I ask, forcing out a happy tone. My gaze drifts to Scott, who's behind Logan, but he isn't looking at us. He is solely fixed on Riot, and he doesn't look happy. In fact, he looks downright pissed, and so he should be.

Riot may be his club brother, but I'm his blood brother.

"Yes. I can't wait to go swimming and go down the swirly slides." He beams up at me.

"Here's his stuff." Scott hands over Logan's bag, and I toss it in the car as Logan climbs into his seat.

I have a child car seat already fitted for him because I never know when I'll have him.

I strap him in and close the door, turning back to my brother.

153

"You, okay?" The little twitch of his head in Riot's direction is enough to tell me why he's asking.

"I am. Thought it would be different, but obviously not," I reply, tucking my hands in my pockets.

The hairs on the back of my neck stand up, alerting me of his closeness. Looking to the side, I see Riot standing there, looking at me. He's still scowling at me, making me frown. Is he pissed at me? He was the one who said all the shitty words.

"You got a sec?" he asks.

His deep voice makes my body shiver as it washes over me. Fucking traitor.

"Not really. I'm busy, just like you are," I snark, before moving around the car and pulling my door open.

He slams the car door shut, and my body goes ridged at how close he is. My anger builds, but I won't let it surface because my nephew is in the car. Turning my head, I look Riot in the eyes.

"What do you want, Riot?"

"We need to talk," he replies.

"No, we don't. Everything was said the other day."

"That wasn't me, baby. Let me explain." His voice is softer this time, but I push the hatred forward, holding on to it.

Turning my body so I'm facing him head-on, I see my brother move in a fraction in case I need him. Riot turns his head to look at Scott and growls.

"Not your business, Mayhem. Back off. This is between my man and me."

"He's my brother before all, Riot. He wants me close; I'll stay close."

They both look at me, and my gaze bounces between the two. Not wanting to cause friction in the club, I shake my head at Scott.

"I'm good. I'll bring Logan home after I take him for some food after swimming. Here or the house?" I ask.

"House. Lizzie will be there. I have shit to do here." I nod, and he walks off.

Turning back to Riot, I see him looking at me, but he doesn't say anything. His beard is longer, his hair is flat, and there are dark circles under his eyes, like he hasn't been sleeping well.

I can hear Logan singing in the car, reminding me that I need to get a move on.

"If you're not going to say anything, I'm going. I promised Logan a fun day, and believe me, this is far from fun."

His eye twitches a little, then he lets out a big sigh and leans against the car.

"What happened the other day, that wasn't me. Have you heard of an angry drunk?" I nod. "A crazy pregnant woman?" I frown.

"Where are you going with this, Riot?"

He sighs, stuffing his hands in his pockets.

"When I'm on painkillers, it makes me have violent tendencies. We found out years ago, which is why I don't touch the stuff. It's pissed me off that none of the brothers, or the doc, warned you beforehand." He shakes his head and looks down at his boots for moment, then focuses back on me. "I know what I said was shitty. I—"

"Obviously the thought was in your head, otherwise you wouldn't have said what you did. I've cleared the air with Chaos, so we're good. I let my fear rule my head for a second. Seeing you hurt made me snap. What I said was disrespectful to the club, but what you said was from the heart. It was hurtful, and it hit its target. The club is a huge part of my life, Riot, always has been, and for you to say I don't know how it works, that hurt me. It cut me deep.

155

"As for you to telling me that no dick, including mine, will tell you what to do, that was the worst. You spoke to me like I was one of the blokes you shag on a weekend. You made me feel small and insignificant. On top of that, I came here today feeling anxious about seeing you, yet I'm once again leaving feeling humiliated after I just watched you laugh and smile with another man, who you let touch you and then kiss you in plain sight. Anyone could have seen you, but clearly you didn't give a fuck about my feelings."

Pulling in a deep breath, I finish off what I need to say so I can leave and start our fun nephew and uncle day.

"This was good while it lasted, Riot, but fucking hell, it's something I will always live by." Once that's said, I pull open the door and get in.

I fasten my seatbelt and go to close the door, but Riot grips the frame. His eyes look sad, and I almost break and pull him to me, but I hold strong. This is something I need to do. I can't keep letting men use me and walk all over me.

"What is?"

"What?" I ask him.

"You said our relationship is something you will live by. What did you mean?" His voice is low, showing his remorse. I look away, hating the look on his face.

Sighing, I sink into my seat and start the car. With my hands gripping the steering wheel, I steel myself.

"I won't ever let a man use me or walk over me again. I learned the hard way that not all people are true to their word, even if they have a good track record," I finish.

I close the door and look at him through the window. I watch as he nods, his gaze drifting to the back window where Logan is calling his name. He smiles at my nephew and waves, before stepping back.

With a deep breath, I pull away, forcing myself not to look in the rear-view mirror. Logan sings in the back seat, as my music plays through the car. He pulls my attention from my heart breaking. I join in singing with him, all the way to the sports centre where we go swimming once a month.

Once parked, I help Logan out, making sure to grab his bag for him. We make our way inside, and I scan my membership card, so we can swim for free. We walk hand in hand to the changing room, and I help Logan strip. He's already wearing his swim shorts under his tracksuit. He sits on the bench as I strip out of my own clothes, also having my swim shorts on underneath.

I tuck our bags into a locker and hook the rubber band with the key around my wrist, then we're walking to the pool area.

Without hesitation, Logan jumps into the kiddie pool, making me laugh as he makes a big splash.

"Kids. Bloody fearless, aren't they?" comes a smooth voice.

Sitting on one of the steps, I turn my head to see a very handsome man looking at me with a smile on his face. He has blonde hair and is clean shaven, with pretty blue eyes. His body is pretty damned good, too.

He's the complete opposite to Riot, and my stomach clenches at the thought, so I push it down. I can't be thinking of him now; comparing other men to him. Shit.

"That they are. Which one is yours?" I ask him.

"That little missy there. She's my niece."

"She's cute. I bring my nephew here once a month," I explain.

"So, you single?" he outright asks me.

I let out a loud mixture of a scoff and a laugh, keeping my eyes focused on Logan, who is splashing and throwing a ball with a few of the kids.

"It's complicated. I—"

"Uncle Ben loves Uncle Riot, don't you," Logan states proudly as he comes to stand in front of us. Damn, this kid has Superman hearing.

"Riot?" the man asks.

Nodding. "Yeah. We're a part of the Road Wreckers MC." The guy's eyes go wide, his eyebrows almost hitting his hairline.

"Oh, wow." Yep, we're used to that reaction.

"So, you're in the club?" he asks me.

"No, my blood brother is—his dad," I tell him. He looks genuinely interested.

"Riot?" he edges again.

"He's the Sargent at Arms for the club."

"And your boyfriend?"

"It's complicated." I shrug and he smiles.

"I heard Daddy telling Lizzie that you were shacking up and in looove, but Uncle Riot was mean to you after he got hurt. But they know he will win you over," he states proudly. He laughs and swims away to the other kids he was playing with.

"I'm telling your dad you were earwigging," I call to him, making him laugh harder.

"He's a smart kid," the man says, and I nod in agreement.

"Way too smart if you ask me." We laugh, then chill out, watching the kids play and splash in the warm water of the pool.

"So, you're gay?" he asks me, and I nod.

"Yeah."

"Me too. Maybe if this thing with this Riot bloke doesn't work out, we could go out for drinks." He sounds hopeful, and I smile at him.

"Maybe." I shrug, not leading him on. I have no idea how this thing with Riot will play out.

"I'm Wayne, by the way."

"Ben." We shake hands and continue to talk.

We watch as the kids play with beach balls and weights, which they drop to the bottom of the pool and play SEALS to dive down and collect them.

Logan is a mini version of his dad, all dark brown, choppy hair with stunning green eyes. He's wicked like him too, always trying new things, having no fear of the unknown. He is someone I love being around, a great kid. My brother did well with him. Plus, he loves Marvel just as much as me.

It's nice to be able to break free from the turmoil that was taking over my thoughts. I have no idea what to do about Riot. His excuse seems plausible. I will have to look into it, maybe even add it into a storyline if it's true.

Not wanting to think about him anymore, I move through the water, on my knees, joining in with the fun and games. When we finally decide to climb out, our new friends join us for some lunch, then we hit the park, making sure the kids are well and truly played out.

We swap numbers but I make sure to tell him we can only be friends because my head is all over the place right now, and I have to sort through everything that's happened. He agrees to be just friends for now—his words, not mine.

Right now, I just need a friend, someone who is not linked to the club in any way.

Twenty-Two

Riot

I slam down the wrench, and it bounces off the floor with a loud clang, being in a sling and working one handed is a fucking cunt plus, watching Ben drive away hours ago was like punch to the gut. Even after I explained everything to him, he still didn't believe me. He just bolted.

Plus, he wouldn't let me explain about Stu. I can't believe he kissed me right as Ben was standing there. Talk about shitty timing. Just my fucking luck that it happened then. It gives him more ammo to hate me.

"Fucking hell," I growl.

"Yeah, you are. I can't believe you would cheat on my brother. Fucking hell, Riot, you knew there was a chance of someone seeing you, of me seeing you. What about Logan? He could have seen it," Mayhem fumes as he closes the gap between us. "And Ben. You knew he was coming to pick the boy up. Is that why you did it? To show him he means nothing—that he was just a fucking game, a challenge?"

I brace for the hit before I even know it's coming, but I *do* know it's coming. He swings his fist, clocking me right in the jaw, and I stumble back, the tool bench behind me stopping me from falling to the floor.

"You really want to do this?" I ask him, standing to my full height.

"Mate, I can go all fucking night. You hurt my brother, so I'm going to hurt you. I told you not to fuck with him if you weren't serious."

"I am serious about him. You know what the pain pills do to me. You should have warned him."

"What about that cunt you were kissing when I walked out?" He pushes against my chest, but I stand firm. I'm bigger than Mayhem, we are evenly matched in a fight, but with my arm in a sling he could win this one.

I push him back with my unhurt arm, and he stumbles back a few feet, giving me room to charge if I need to. But I really fucking hope it doesn't come to that. My feet spread, balancing myself out, ready to brace again if needed.

"That was Stu. He's a guy I shagged on the regular a year ago, but he left—until last week when he came back and sought me out. I told him about Ben and the shit that happened the other day. Stu said he thought it wasn't serious since we weren't talking, and he kissed me."

"Yeah well, you didn't exactly push him away, brother. Ben saw it all, and so did I. Luckily for you, Logan was focused on my brother."

"It shocked me, okay? Fuck, mate, I'm only human," I gripe, rubbing the back of my neck as my body relaxes a little.

Mayhem is a conniving cunt when he wants to be, he'll do just about anything to get what he wants.

"Listen, I want Ben. I claimed him. He's my old man, and he will be my husband. Maybe we'll even adopt. The thing is, Ben is a stubborn bastard, just like someone else I know." I cock an eyebrow in challenge.

He smirks at me, and I know we're okay. That's the way we work: we bitch, we fight, and then we are good.

"He'll make me work for him, and I'm fully prepared to do that."

161

He says nothing as we stand in this face-off. Minutes tick by and no words are spoken. We're both pissed but for different reasons. Him because he thinks I cheated on Ben; me because both him and Ben don't trust me. I know what Ben saw, but he didn't give me the benefit of the doubt.

Mayhem's eye twitches, but then his body relaxes, and mine follows suit.

"I am warning you now, brother. You hurt him again and I will burying you in so many fucking graves, they will never piece you back together. You got me?"

I nod. "No need for a warning, brother. I will end myself before I ever hurt him again."

With a nod, he walks over to the main door, but doesn't walk in.

"Get in here, fucker. We need a drink—or ten." He winks at me and pulls the door open.

Smiling, I shake my head and follow him inside. He is already at the bar, lining up shots with Chaos, Psycho and a few of the other brothers standing around him. Walking over to my brothers, my family, I smile as they all look at me with a shot raised in the air.

"To Riot, the club's SAA. The one prick who likes pricks, but his drugged-up mouth runs away with him." Chaos salutes me, and everyone cheers with him.

We drink and drink. Shot after shot, they go down. We talk, laugh, and drink the rest of the day. When the sun goes down, we move from the main room out into the back garden part of the compound. Sitting on a range of mixed chairs, we carry on our bonding into the night.

"Fuck, I'm seeing double," I laugh.

"Man, I am blacking the fuck out," I hear someone slur.

"Oh, fuck," I hear, and we all look over to see that Keys has fallen off his chair, which is now half lying on top of him. His laughter turns into a snore, and we all burst out laughing again.

These are my brothers, my family. My foggy brain tries to sift through my past and imagine my future. The club is always front and centre, now with the addition of Ben. My good mood abruptly fades when I remember the pain and anger on his handsome face. It was me who put that look there; my words, my actions.

"Fucking hell," I mutter to no one.

I look around the group of fuckers I call family and see them talking—well, slurring their words. We recant old stories; we talk about the shit we want in the future of the club. Not sure what we will remember tomorrow, but at least tomorrow will come.

One of the prospects is looking around the grounds, still on guard, and I have to hand it to him, he's doing good with not drinking. He's protecting his club. Good man.

Ben is a good man. He's too fucking good for me but fuck me I can't let him go. I know he could find a nice boy to settle down with, someone as intelligent as him, someone who won't get shot at, or arrested and sent to jail.

I groan and bring the bottle of Fireball to my lips, downing the rest of it, before dropping it to the floor. Letting out a loud burp, I get to my feet and step over to Mayhem, kicking his booted foot. He looks up at me with eyes as glassy as my own.

"What, cuntface?" he slurs.

His head lulls to the side as he waits for me to speak. Licking my dry lips, I bend down, almost head butting him when I stumble forward.

"Fuck. Why are you got to trying to kiss me, brother? It's Benny Boy you love, not me."

Shit. Everything is spinning. I try to focus. Did he just say I love Ben? Nah, fuck if he did.

"Ben is mine. His arse is mine." I hiccup and carry on, "I want him and no one will stop me."

I straighten my spine—well, I think I do; everything is messed up thanks to the copious amount of alcohol we have drunk tonight. These boys joined me in drowning my situation, helping to make me forget for a while.

"Then do something about it, Leo," Mayhem says, using my birth name.

"I will."

"Good."

"Fine."

"Fine," he mutters sleepily. Looking down at him, I see he has slipped into a lazy sleep, and I smile, kicking him again. But the prick doesn't move.

"You two are like a bunch of teenage girls. Fuck off with that shit," Psycho gripes, before bringing his bottle to his lips and taking a drink.

"Wanker," I reply, and walk away from them, into the clubhouse. Stumbling down the hall to my room, I push my door open and fall face down on my bed.

Ben's face invades my drunken brain, making me smile before the sleepy darkness takes me.

I crack an eye open and wince. Holy mother of God, that hurts like a bitch. Slamming my eye shut, I force my head to face away from the sunlight that's coming through my window.

My mouth feels like a desert and tastes like arse. Why the hell did I drink so much last night? Fuck me.

Moaning, I roll over. I sling my legs over the side of the bed and stumble into my bathroom to take a leak. To purge the rest of the alcohol from my body. I have no doubt that my liver is in a coma from the abuse I put it through last night.

When I finish, I flush and jump in the shower, hoping the cold water will wake me up. Well, it's either a kill or cure. I cringe when the cold water first hits my body, almost shrieking like a girl, but I bite my tongue.

Quickly washing my body and hair, I climb out and wrap a towel around my waist. Stepping into my room, I look down at the bed and see images of Ben there, battered and bruised, but then I see images of him in his bed as I fucked him. I love seeing him ready and wating for me.

Love?

Shit, what was it Mayhem said last night? That I love Ben? Do I?

It dawns on me that yeah, I fucking do love him.

I would do anything to protect him. Anything he needs or wants; I will get it for him.

But when it comes to romance and all that chicky stuff, I'm crap at it. I'll need to rope in the old ladies to help with winning him over, because I know he wants me—hell, he even might love me. I saw the pain I caused in his eyes. Surely that isn't an emotion from someone who was just happy to let me fuck them.

Knowing what I have to do, I get dressed, not bothering to style my hair or shave. Collecting my shit, I rush from my room and to the kitchen, because first off, I need coffee. Strong, black coffee.

To my surprise, every one of my brothers are in the kitchen, drinking coffee and shovelling food into their mouths, which the prospects have cooked.

Moving over to the counter, I pick up a mug and fill it to the brim, then stir in three sugars. I let the hot liquid slide down my throat, before I move over to the table and sit, then pile breakfast onto a plate.

"How you feeling?" Chaos asks from his seat.

"Like a road sweeper moved into my head," I mutter.

Everyone chuckles. We eat and talk in hushed tones because clearly everyone is struggling this morning. Thank fuck I don't work on Sundays.

"Brothers," Psycho states, walking into the room.

"Fucker never suffers," Mayhem grumbles, making Psycho chuckle.

"I need your old ladies," I state, and everyone goes deathly silent and looks at me.

"What the fuck?"

"You like cock and arse, fucker."

"Hell no," they all bitch at the same time.

Holding my hands up in mock surrender, I laugh. They are all still scowling at me, throwing daggers through their eyes at me.

"Listen, I need advice from your women. I need to win Ben back, and I'm shit at all that romantic crap. You all know how much I fucked up." I shake my head, bringing the pain of my hangover back. "Jesus, I think I'm still drunk from last night because I can't believe I am asking you bunch of crazy-arse motherfuckers for advice on my love life."

The men snicker behind their coffee mugs. Mayhem winks at me and I flip the prick off.

"I'll call the women in. But be warned, they are gunning for your blood after what you did to Ben."

"Fucking hell." I sigh. "You are all acting like he caught me fucking someone else."

"Well, it wouldn't be the first time, would it," Chaos pipes in.

Shaking my head at him, I get to my feet. They are pissing me off; no fucking help whatsoever. Cunts.

166

"Fuckers. I'm out. I'll sort my own shit out. Thanks for nothing," I whine like a petulant child. I storm out of the clubhouse and mount my bike, then fasten my helmet before pulling away from the compound and hitting the motorway. I need to clear my head.

The wind rushes over my body, clearing away the hangover fog and the thoughts of Ben.

I need a plan, and going to the old ladies will just add to my headache, so I will do this shit on my own. I mean, I'm Riot, the SAA of the Road Wreckers MC. Fuck what they all think. I will get back in Ben's good books, and he will let me fuck him again because I know how much he likes my cock in him. Not cocky, but the truth.

A plan forms in my head and I smile, knowing Ben won't know what hit him. Bring on Tuesday.

Twenty-Three

Ben

It's been two days since I saw Riot kissing some other guy. He hasn't tried to text or call me again and I'm both happy because I need some space and disappointed that he isn't fighting for me.

I have resigned myself to the idea that what happened between us didn't mean as much to him as it did me.

"Oh, I'm so happy you agreed to come with us, Ben." I smile at Glenna, one of the authors I'm meeting up with for a coffee today.

Glenna is here with Tia, Ally and Martin.

They have been trying for a while now to get me to meet up and I've always dodged their attempts. But now I'm attending my first author event and possibly moving into the romance genre, I thought it would be a good idea to meet up face to face and have a chat.

"Me, too. It has been a long time coming," I agree and sip my tea.

"Definitely. I mean, if you're crossing over to the dark side with us, into the sexy scenes and very hot covers, then yes, we need to chat and offer advice. I mean, I'm sure you need help looking for a hot cover model." Tia winks at me, making me chuckle.

"True. I have seen some and they're hot," I reply.

"So do you have a special man in your life?" Ally asks.

Shaking my head, I explain, "It is complicated. I thought we had something going but it turned out to be nothing."

"Aww, I'm sorry honey," she replies, laying her hand on top of mine and giving it a squeeze. I shrug.

"It is what it is. I've known him for years, so I knew what I was getting into when we started something."

"Well, he's a fool for letting you go," Martin chimes in.

These people are amazing. Even though we've only talked online for a while, and this is our first time meeting face to face, it seems like it's a weekly occurrence with how easy the conversation flows.

"Anyway, no more of the heavy lovey stuff. Let's move on to cover models," Tia states, redirecting the conversation.

"Oh, shush you. You just like looking at the half-naked men," Martin says, smiling at her.

"Oh, hell yes, and speaking of half-naked men. I would love to see what *he* looks like naked," Tia says with wide eyes, looking over my shoulder.

"Holey Moley, yes. He belongs on a sexy MC cover."

Twisting in my seat, I look behind me and see Riot walking past the window. He looks at me and winks, a huge grin on his face. He's in faded black jeans, and has a white t-shirt on under his leather jacket that shows off his club patches with pride. I also spot the rainbow badge below his name.

We stay locked on each other as he keeps walking toward the door. He breaks the connection as he holds the door open for a couple of ladies to walk through. I remotely hear my friends gush over his actions and how he looks. Great.

"Shit," I mutter under my breath as he walks into the café, toward our table.

Tia snaps her head in my direction, frowning, then her lips split into a huge smile as she realises who he is. I nod and sink back into my chair.

"Ohmygod," she mouths, and I nod, pressing my lips together to stop me from smiling.

Riot stops next to the table, keeping his gaze locked on mine. His hands hang loosely at his sides, giving him that relaxed feel, which I am anything but right now.

"Well, hello, handsome, can we help you with anything?" Glenna asks Riot, who is looking at me, not paying anyone else any attention.

Riot blinks and tears his eyes from mine to look down at the kooky woman. He gives her a blinding smile.

"I can think of something. Maybe you can help me win my man back. You see, I fucked up. Said some shit I didn't mean. Then he saw something that was taken the wrong way. I am a biker after all, and we mess up. What would you suggest I do?" he asks, his voice calm.

Everyone is looking at me, except Glenna, who is still eye-fucking Riot. I smirk at the look in her eyes. Finally, she speaks, and looks to the chair between her and me. He taps it.

"Well, lucky for you, we all know a thing or two about love and men that fuck it up. So, take a seat and we will see what we can do to help." Riot steps around the table, his eyes once again finding mine.

He sits next to me, making sure to brush his thigh against mine, sending shivers over my body. I grip the mug in my hand so hard I think it might crack under the pressure.

"Hi," he says.

Turning my head, I look at him. I mean really look at him. Damn, he's handsome, though his beard is a little longer and he still looks tired. My heart skips a beat at seeing him this close. It's only been two days since I last saw him, yet I've missed him, even though he hurt me.

My workload has been happy with the distance between us because it's what I do: I throw myself into my work when I'm feeling angry, hurt, or pissed at people. I can see plenty of work being done in my future, with or without Riot.

This man evokes so many emotions in me. He's like my very own personal roller-coaster.

"Hi," I reply. His hand finds my thigh and my body jerks at the touch.

He grins at me as his fingers flex on my leg, then he's sliding them closer to my dick, which is chubbing out. I lick my lips, drawing his gaze down to my mouth, and I see his body sway forward, like he's going to kiss me. Suddenly, he looks up and stops moving, like he just remembered where we are and the fact we are on the outs right now.

Even though we're broken up, the sexual chemistry between us is off the charts. My body misses his touch; the feel of his skin against mine; his beard running over my mouth when he kisses me.

"So, what's your name?" Ally asks, breaking the sexual tension between us.

I blink, and so does Riot as he pulls back.

"Riot," is all he says.

"Is that your real name or a nickname?" Martin asks him.

I look around the table and find everyone is watching Riot, all except Tia, who is watching me. She gives me a small smile because she knows what he is, or was, to me.

"It's my road name. I'm a member of the Road Wreckers MC, just like Ben's brother, Mayhem," he explains, and they all nod and gush.

"Ooh, so you know each other"? Martin asks, before taking a sip of his coffee.

"Yeah, you could say that," Riot replies. I can feel his stare on the side of my face, but I refuse to look at him.

My friends pepper Riot with questions, while his hand rests on my thigh. The heat from his palm seeps through the

171

denim and into my skin, marking me. I swallow hard, reaching for my mug of tea, which is most likely cold now. Taking a sip, I ignore the awful taste of the lukewarm liquid and place my mug back down. I jump when Riot's hand tightens on my thigh.

My head snaps in his direction, a frown on my face. His gaze bores into mine, but he doesn't say anything, so Tia fills me in on why he looks so pissed right now.

"We were just telling Riot that you're looking at putting a shirtless model on the cover of your next book and talking about the possibility of you having a custom photoshoot with a model." She winks at me.

"Oh, yeah," I mutter, shocked she told him that.

Why would she tell him that? We didn't talk about a photoshoot. Fuck, no wonder he looks like he's ready to rip someone's head off. He thinks I'm going to be working with half naked men.

Why would he care? He was more than happy to bitch me out and kiss other men. So why can't I do a photoshoot with another guy?

Riot moves closer, placing his mouth close to my ear, his stubble rubbing against the outer shell, and my body responds to the slight contact. Images of how that stubble felt brushing up and down my cock, flood my mind. Shit.

"You won't be looking at any naked men, Ben. You belong to me, so don't pull this shit," he grinds out.

"Aww," someone gushes.

I turn my head a little, until we are almost nose to nose. I can feel his breath on my lips, causing me to lick them.

His eyes are dark, filled with lust and anger, but I know he would never hurt me—well, not physically anyway. Shit, he's hurt me emotionally, and I know I shouldn't have let that happen because I knew who he was when I stepped into this relationship. Maybe we jumped too soon. We should have

172

taken the time to talk and get to know each other on a deeper level than we have grown accustomed to over the years.

"Do I? Was it not your mouth that was on another guy's mouth a few days ago? Was it not you who told me the club comes before anyone? Didn't you tell me that no dick would ever tell you what to do? That, to me, doesn't sound like I belong to you, Riot, nor that you belong to me. That sounds like you got what you wanted, completed the challenge, then took the easy way out."

He doesn't say anything for a short time, just keeps looking at me. My friends don't say or do anything. They just take in the scene. If they're like me, they will be taking mental notes of how things are playing out.

"You want to do this here?" he asks in a low tone, and I shrug.

No, I don't want to do this here, but I'm not one to back down. This has been building for a few days, and because we haven't spoken, I've had no outlet. Not that he hasn't tried to contact me, but I wasn't in a good enough head space to duke it out with him.

"I've explained what happened with the painkillers. That was not my fault." I go to cut him off, but he holds his hand up to stop me. "No, it's my turn. You got yours at the clubhouse the other day, before you ran. Someone should have warned you about my reaction. As for what you saw, he kissed me. He's back in town, and yes, we used to fuck. A lot. I told him we were together, and I told him we weren't talking because of some shit. He took that to mean we weren't serious, and he kissed me, which you saw."

"Maybe you think it happened like that, Riot, but I watched the whole thing play out. He touched your arm, then kissed you, and you didn't push him away. You let him kiss you. Maybe because you wanted it, I don't know, but fuck me, that was like a kick to the balls."

173

Getting to my feet, I pull my leather jacket off the back of my chair and look to my friends, forcing a smile.

"It was wicked meeting you all, but I have to go. I'll chat to you all later." They nod and give me smiles, then I leave.

I can hear his boots thumping across the floor of the café, but I don't turn around. Walking through the door, I make my way to my car, which is parked in the car park just around the corner.

"Ben, fucking stop, for fuck's sake," he calls to me.

I stop when I get to my car, turning to look at him. He steps closer and my body responds to the idea of him getting close enough to touch, to kiss.

"Say what you have to say, Riot. I need to get home and do some work," I state.

"What, are you in a rush to look at naked men to go on a cover, or to pick a guy you want to get naked and front of you?" he snarks off, making me grin at the sudden jealousy coming from him.

"You jealous, Riot?" I cross my arms over my chest, really liking the look on his face.

He looks annoyed as fuck. His lips thin and his nostrils flare as he glares at me.

He steps closer, his feet landing on the outside of mine, caging me in. His sandalwood scent invades my senses, and I have to hold back a groan.

"Damn straight I am. I'm the only bloke you get to see naked, Ben, and I'm the only man you *will* see naked. No other fucker gets to see this." He waves his hand down his body.

"Since when? If my memory serves me right, many, and I mean *many,* guys have seen you naked, Riot," I reply.

My arms drop to my sides as he closes the small gap between us until his chest touches mine. I can feel the bulge in his jeans as it presses against me.

174

Licking my lips, I watch as his gaze drops to my mouth, then travels back up my face to look me in the eye. With his hands on my car behind me, he presses his groin into me, so we are flush from hips to chest. Cock to cock.

"Everyone before you doesn't exist. They were a warm body to fill in the time before I got you in my bed and on the back of my bike. Mark my words, Ben, you are my old man, and no fucker will take you from me. I may fuck up from time to time, but what do you expect? I'm a biker, for fuck's sake. But I know you will reel me in when I go too far. This..." He looks down to where we are pressed together, then back up to my face. "This is happening. Fucking up is what I do, but I'm awesome enough to admit it and help you forget and move on. Speaking of moving on, I'll pick you up tonight, at eight. We can go out for some food and a drink. I need to do some collections first, and then I'm all yours." He leans in and kisses me like there's no tomorrow.

His tongues dominates mine as he takes what he wants. My hands find his waist, my fingers hooking into the belt loops of his jeans and holding him to me.

All too soon he's breaking the kiss and stepping back from me with a sexy grin on his face.

"Later," is all he says, then he's turning on his heel and walking away, leaving me a gooey mess in a public car park with a raging hard-on and heavy balls.

Fuck my life with a cricket bat.

Twenty-Four

Riot

I'm not one for dates, but knowing Ben likes them made me decide to take the step. When I was looking for where to take him, I was told he likes pub food, and I'm all up for that. I don't do fancy shit, and I know Ben is the same.

We like beer and steak.

"How's the food?" I ask him, before taking a pull from my beer.

He's sitting across from me in a booth at a pub I found that has good food reviews. He's eating a steak and ale pie with mash, peas, and gravy. Me—I went with a huge surf 'n' turf with chips.

"It's good," is all he says.

I watch as he looks around the room, people watching. It's something he often does. He says it helps him take mental notes on how people are. Sometimes he uses their mannerisms for a character.

"Just good? Come on, Ben, is this how it's going to be? I make an effort and it gets thrown back in my fucking face? I'm trying here, you know," I spit out.

I push my plate away, losing my appetite. Settling back into the booth, I down the rest of my beer, not looking at Ben, who I can feel watching me.

I thought he would have had time to let my words from this afternoon sink in, but clearly he's as stubborn as his brother and nephew. Shaking my head, I push down the tightening of my gut. I pull out my wallet and try to signal for the waiter to bring me the bill.

"What do you want me to say, Riot? I'm trying too. It gutted me when I saw him kiss you. How would you feel if I walked up to the bar and kissed someone right now?"

A growl emanates from my chest and out between my lips before I can stop it. Ben smiles and cocks an eyebrow at me.

"Point proven," he says to me.

"So, you want to go and kiss someone else, or see some other guy naked? You want to play me?" I snarl. His smile drops, and I know I just fucked up again.

"No, I don't, Leo. I would never do that. Tia was winding you up because she clocked who you were. Yes, I will be putting a half-naked model on my cover. Will I meet him? Probably not. But sex sells and having a sexy cover will help get the book attention. Fuck, if it's going to cause so much trouble, then you be on it," he snaps at me.

"You want other people drooling over this on your book?" I drag my hand down my body with a smirk on my face.

I watch as his eyes dilate, then darken with lust for me. Yeah, he's getting turned on at the thought of people eye-fucking me when they can't have me, because I'm his.

Blinking, he shrugs. "It could work. Maybe I'll ask the other members to be on a cover too. I'm planning on a four, maybe five book series," he explains, and I nod.

"I'll help in any way I can, baby. You know that."

He smiles at me, his eyes softening when I call him 'baby'. It's been a while since I've done that. Recently, I've kept to his birth name.

"I am sorry for what went down. I never meant to hurt you, Ben. You have to know that. I'm not good at all this

177

shit. I'm used to shagging and leaving. It's what I do. But I will try for you." He winces at my words, but they needed to be said.

"I knew what you were like going into this, Leo, but it hit me the other day just how much you could ruin me." Sitting back in his seat, Ben watches me as I study him.

This is one thing we like to do: watch each other.

"You can do the same to me, Ben. We're men, and we fuck up. It's in our DNA. But, baby, we'll learn together. So… are you in or out?"

Licking his lips, he leans forward, his forearms resting on the table that separates us, linking his fingers together.

"In," he says. "But no more chances. You mess up, I'm done. You may fuck me like no other has before, but I will find a mediocre stand-in for you, and you, Leo Peters, will have to see me with him for the rest of your life. So, who I fuck in the future is in your hands," he smarts off, looking damned proud of himself.

"That's it? No bitching or making demands?" I ask him. He shakes his head.

"No. You have explained what happened, and we talked it over. I'm not one to drag shit out, Leo. If we want this, we take it. You've heard my warning." He winks.

Biting my lip, I groan. My cock grows hard in my jeans, pressing against the metal zipper that is no doubt leaving marks on my bare cock, because I don't wear boxers. I like going commando, for my balls to be free.

Ben's eyes narrow on me, dark and needy. I smirk at him and he gives me a sly grin, letting me know exactly what he's thinking.

"I'm going to pay the bill. Meet me at my bike. I need to be balls deep inside your arse, baby. Go." I nod to the exit and, thank fuck, he listens.

I rush over to the bar and pay the bill, then practically run from the pub, finding Ben leaning against my bike, his ankles crossed, arms folded over his chest. The leather jacket he's wearing looks hot as fuck. He's looking down at his phone, smiling.

He hears me approach and shows me the screen. It's a photo of one of his friends covered in paint.

"Shouldn't there be more paint on the wall than on her?" I ask, laughing.

"Apparently not." He gets on the bike behind me, his cock pressing against the small of my back as his hands settle on my dick, which is trying to break through the denim to get to him.

We ride in the direction of Ben's house, and with each mile that passes, his hold on my dick tightens and his cock hardens against my back, sending my need for him into maximum overdrive. Fuck, I need to bury myself in him before I crash my bike and potentially kill us both.

Seeing a sign for a farm, I indicate and pull onto the road leading to it. It's lined with high bushes and trees. Going far enough down the narrow lane so we can't be seen from the main road, I pull into to a small layby and kill the bike's engine.

I climb off, removing my helmet and thanking the road gods that Ben is doing the same. He has a sly grin on his face, like he's read my mind.

Taking his face in my hands, I bring my mouth to his, kissing the fuck out of him. With our lips still attached, Ben manages to swing his leg over my bike, resting his feet either side of mine.

We grope at each other while kissing, our tongues fighting for dominance. My lips travel from his mouth down to his jaw, nipping at his beard. I love seeing him tense and moan at the bite. Kissing his neck, I suck on the skin, marking him as he rocks his cock against mine.

"I want you. Now," I say against his neck, and he nods, not saying anything.

Pulling back, I spin him around, bending him over, his arse on view for me. Arching his back, I take in the scene before me and let out a deep moan, causing Ben to look at me over his shoulder with a sexy grin on his lips.

"Like what you see, handsome?" he asks.

Stepping close, I move my hands around his waist, undoing his button and pulling down the zip of his jeans, then tug them down his thighs, along with his boxers.

"There's no lube, but I'll make it work," I say, and he nods.

"Do it. I need you in me. I've missed you, Leo."

Sucking on my fingers, I make them nice and wet before pulling his arse cheeks apart, then slide my fingers over his tight hole. With my other hand, I pull my cock out of my jeans, through the zipper. Ben hisses at the intrusion as I slide my finger into him; slowly at first, then when he begins to relax, I thrust harder and faster.

"Oh, shit, yes," he moans.

"You want my cock, baby?" I ask.

"Yes," he pants out. Smirking at his back, I pull his arse cheeks apart. I spit on his tight hole, making sure he's nice and wet, ready for me to slide into him, and all the while I don't let up with my finger, getting rougher with every thrust in preparation for him to take me.

Standing back up with my cock in hand, I remove my finger from him and guide the head to his hole, before slowly pushing in.

We both moan at the contact, at the way he tightens around my cock, strangling it, sucking me in and wanting more. Once I've pushed all the way in, Ben lets out a loud sigh, then starts to push back against me.

"Fuck, that's sexy. Fuck me back, baby. Hell yeah, do it." And he does.

I adjust my stance and brace against his thrusts as he slides up and down my thick shaft. Over and over again I watch my dick disappear into his tight hole, each of us breathing heavily from the sexually charged moment.

Fuck me, my man is sexy as shit. He can and will do whatever he wants to me and with me. Ben Miller is perfect for me. He knows how I like it, and I know how he likes to fuck. Seeing him fuck me so eagerly outside, where we could be caught any second, makes me want to explode.

At that thought, my balls tighten, and Ben starts to pant more harshly. I can feel him tightening around me, and I know he's close.

"Wank that cock, Ben. Come for me, baby," I growl as my balls draw up and my orgasm hits. "Yesss." I drag out the word as I fill him up.

"Fuck. Shit, Riot. Oh hell, Leo, I'm—" Ben's sentence ends on a groan as he comes.

Resting my head on his back, we both pant, catching our breaths. Birds chirp close by, and cows moo in the field. Ben laughs, and I can't stop from chuckling with him.

"Do you think they enjoyed the show?" Ben asks.

"No doubt. I'm going to pull out." He nods, and I slowly withdraw my softening cock from his arse. He winces, then lets out a slow sigh.

I tuck my wet cock back into my jeans, noting that we need a shower when we get to his place—as well as round two. Looking down, I see my cum leak out of his arse, and my cock jerks. Greedy prick.

"Fuck me, that's a sight to see," I mutter, keeping my eyes focussed on his arse cheeks.

"Dirty bastard," Ben mutters and pulls his jeans up, not caring that my cum will soak into his boxers and jeans.

"You love it." I smirk at him and lean in for a kiss.

"I do." My heart stutters at his words. His eyes bore into mine, and I can't say anything, so I kiss him. Words are lodged in my throat, but I hope this kiss says what I can't—yet.

"Come on, let's get to your place, shower, and prepare for round two. I want to take my time with you," I tell him.

He smiles and gets on my bike, adjusting his helmet. Once I've put my own on, I straddle my bike and start her up. Ben's hands rest on my hips, holding me as I pull away and ride back to the main road, toward his house.

The need to have him again builds as we get closer to his house.

Seeing his place come into view, my cock goes steel hard. Pulling back on the throttle, I gun it to get there quicker. As soon as my bike comes to a stop, Ben is off it, removing his helmet, and rushing toward his front door.

I grin and swing my leg over, taking my own helmet off. When I catch up to him, I see his body is tight and shaking. Something is off.

"Baby?" I try, but he doesn't respond. "Ben?" I say louder as I get to him.

He looks at me over his shoulder, then down to the floor in front of him. Frowning, I step to his side, and growl at what I find.

There, on his doorstep, is a dead rat, blood seeping from its prone body. It's eyes have been gouged out, and its front and back legs look bent out of shape.

"What the fuck?" Pulling on Ben, I make him look at me. "Go to my bike. I need to call Prez, okay?"

He nods, looking back at the dead animal. Ben is a softy when it comes to animals. Fuck, he won't kill a damned spider.

He listens and goes to my bike, and as soon as he's out of earshot, I unlock my phone and call Chaos.

"Riot," he greets.

"We have a situation. I need to put Ben in lockdown."

Twenty-five

Ben

Logan sits next to me in the main room at the clubhouse, where I'm on lockdown for who knows how long. Two nights ago, someone left a dead, mutilated rat on my doorstep. Seeing it made my stomach churn. I love animals, no matter what species they are, and seeing that made me want to vomit.

Riot jumped into action and brought me to the clubhouse, where the club can keep an eye on me. Not only was Riot pissed about the rat, but so was my brother and the other men of the club. They know I can handle myself when needed, but they took this as a genuine threat, especially since I took that beating not long ago.

Psycho thinks it's Harry being all dramatic, and to be fair, he could be right.

I've also received texts and emails with dark, sick images of dead animals. Satanic images, blooded dolls heads, just general twisted shit. But they all have one thing in common: death.

Shaking the thoughts from my head, I look over at my nephew, who is playing on his tablet. I smile and run my fingers through his hair, but he doesn't acknowledge me doing it; too engrossed in his the game. Looking around the room, I watch as some of the brothers play cards, drinking and having a laugh.

My brother throws his head back, laughing at whatever Chaos just told him, Psycho and Riot.

Riot is looking sexy as fuck with a glass of whisky in one hand and a cigar in the other, his ankle resting on his knee. His jeans look tight around his thighs, the white t-shirt he's wearing under his black cut gives him that edgy biker image. Damn, that would be a sexy book cover.

As if sensing me looking at him, he brings his gaze to mine, smirking when he sees me eye-fucking him. When he throws me a wink, I smile and reach down to my crotch, adjusting my thickening dick. Riot cocks an eyebrow at me and I shrug.

Winking at him, I look down at my laptop and start working on the first biker book in my new series. Being around the club and its members, I know how things work, and I will try to be as true to that world as possible.

My little chat with Chaos about the new MC series was good, informative. It also set boundaries for me. Chaos doesn't care that the books will be MC, but he wants me to keep the guys' names out of it, plus any detail that might be linked to the club.

A shadow casts over me, and I don't have to look up to know it's Riot. Keeping my eyes fixed on the screen, I smile to myself when he just stands there doing nothing for a few seconds. Then I feel it.

He grabs the back of my neck, pulling me back and attacking my mouth with a kiss so deep I feel it in my bones, and my cock and balls respond in an instant. Cheering goes up around the room, making me smile against his lips.

"Ewww, you're like Dad and Lizzie," Logan protests from his seat.

"You'll be kissing girls in no time, little man," Riot tells him, and Logan looks shocked by that. Then his face twists like he sucked on a lemon.

"Eww, no. No kissing for me," he states, getting to his knees. "Since you like Riot again, does that mean we can't go swimming and get food with Wayne and Chloe anymore?"

I feel Riot stiffen next to me, and I can't help but smile. Scott looks at me and grins, shaking his head as he takes the seat across from me and Logan.

"Tell me, Logan, who is this, '*Wayne*'?" Riot's voice is firm yet holds a light tone because he's talking to a kid.

He perches on the arm of the sofa I'm sitting on, keeping his hand firmly on my neck. The smile that brightens up my nephew's face has Riot's fingers flexing against my body. He knows that Logan and I are close, so seeing this kid happy for us, makes my heart swell, but I think it scares Riot, because Logan can be a little shit when he wants to be. By this time, Chaos and Psycho have joined us, as have the women.

They like to seek out the juicy gossip. They each give me a smile and take a seat, and my brother pulls Lizzie into his lap.

"Me and Uncle Ben met them when we went swimming. We swam and played, then we went for some food. I had chicken nuggets and chips! Then Wayne bought us ice cream. We're doing it again, and Uncle Ben said that one day we can go to the Jungle Bungle."

"Wow, that sounds like fun. How about your Uncle Ben and I take you instead?"

Logan's face lights up, and he jumps to his feet, clapping. I love that Riot wants to spend time with him. He's a big part of my life. Not only that, but I have to laugh at the fact he's trying to one-up a man I met once and spent a total of four hours with.

"Awesome!" he yells, and then he's off; climbing over me to get to Riot. Lowering his voice, he whispers, "I don't think

Uncle Ben liked Wayne the way he likes you. They didn't kiss or anything."

I hold my breath and the women gasp, but the men laugh behind their hands. I scowl at them, which only makes them laugh louder, no longer trying to hide it. Great, just great. Looking up at Riot, I see he's holding Logan on his lap, looking down at this five-year-old kid with narrowed eyes.

"Payback is a bitch, brother," Keys calls out.

Riot flips him off behind Logan's back, then sets the boy down on his feet, ruffling his hair.

"Thanks for the info, kid." His voice is deep, gravelly, and my body shivers from the sound. "My room. Now," he states, not even looking at me before walking off.

I look around at everyone and see they're all smirking and smiling. Shaking my head, I flip them off.

"Prospect, turn the music up. We don't need to hear that shit," Chaos calls.

As I walk away, I hear Logan asking what shit is and why they don't want to hear it.

Making my way down the hall to Riot's room, my heart pounds. I saw how pissed he was, but he hid it from my nephew. His voice also went deep like it does when he's turned on.

His door is open when I get there, and he's lying on the bed. He has removed his boots, socks, t-shirt and cut. When I enter, managing to get just inside the door, before I can say anything, he snaps, "Close the door and lock it."

"Okay, bossy," I snark off, knowing it will piss him off more.

I bet a pissed off Riot will fuck like a beast, and that's something I want right now. The things that man can and will do to me makes for very happy wet dreams, and I've had plenty over the years.

"Bossy? You haven't seen anything yet, babe. Now strip."

Doing as he says, I turn from the door, removing my t-shirt from my body then dropping it to the floor. He undoes his jeans and lifts his arse off the bed a fraction to push them down his legs. Kicking them off, he takes his cock in hand, running his palm up and down his thick shaft.

He watches as I tug down my joggers, sans boxers today. Stepping over to the bed, I kneel and lean over, keeping my gaze locked on him, and lick the head of his cock. A drop of precum bubbles there and seeps into my taste buds, making me want more.

"More than lick it, babe. Suck me all the fucking way down. I want to see you choke on *my* cock, not some prick's who tried picking you up at the pool," he grinds out, and I smirk at him.

I knew it was jealousy that brought us to his room, with him acting like this, and I like it. I really fucking like it. Positioning myself between his thighs, I grip the base of his dick and open my mouth wide, before sliding him in inch by inch.

He hisses, and I grin around his thick shaft, my cock twitching.

His hand rests on the back of my head, pushing me down, but not enough for panic to set in. Using my tongue, I tease the vein that runs along the underside. He hisses and grinds out my name.

"Yeah, that's it, Ben. Take all of it."

My mouth tightens around him as the small amount of pubic hair he has tickles my lips. Breathing through my nose, I allow Leo to hold me in place while he thrusts into my mouth in short bursts. The whole thing turns me on to no end, and I leak all over the bedding. He's been bossy in bed, but he has never been this rough before.

I love it.

He lets me go in a flash, and I sit up, gasping for air, before he ushers me back on his cock. After repeating the same thing, once, then twice, he finally gives me a reprieve. He pulls me up his body, taking my swollen mouth in a searing kiss that takes the last bit of breath I had in me.

"Fuck me, that was some sexy shit to watch. Seeing my cock completely vanish inside of your mouth, then to feel your throat tighten around me… Holy shit, I almost came, baby. But I want to come in your arse. Turn around and present that fine hole to me."

Listening to him, I shift on the bed. My knees are by his hips, my arse close to his face, and the head of my cock almost touches his chest. With my hands braced on the bed, I hold myself up, even though my limbs go weak when he swipes his tongue over my arsehole.

A deep moan slips from my throat. "Oh, shit."

I can feel him smile against my body, and then he's prodding me with his tongue, his fingers flexing against my arse cheeks. I rock back and forth on his face, not giving a fuck.

He makes me feel sexy and wanted.

Riot brings out the primal in me.

He doesn't keep me waiting long before fingers are digging into me, stretching me enough to take his cock again, which is very quickly becoming my favourite thing with him. I love the feel of him deep inside of me.

"I need you in me, Leo. Please," I beg, my voice sounding needy.

"You will fucking have me, baby. Turn around. I want you to ride me." Half crawling off his lap, I turn around and straddle his lap, the hairs from his thighs tickling mine.

Our cocks rub together, and pre-cum links us as it strings between each shaft. The sight is bloody magnificent. I lean over to get my phone from the bedside table and open the camera app, then smile at Leo, who's grinning at me. He knows what I want.

Aiming the camera at our dicks, I click. In the photo you can see the string of cum connecting us together. It's erotic but also symbolic for me; for us. The picture looks amazing, like some porn image that people pay thousands for.

"Send that to me," he growls, his hands engulfing both our dicks as he starts wanking us both off.

I moan as I quickly send the photo to him, then drop my phone back onto the bedside table. My head drops back as the sensation of our dicks rubbing together washes over me.

"Get on me," Leo growls, and the sound sends my body into shivers.

Spitting on his hand, he rubs the wetness against my hole, then grips the base of his dick, lining it up for me to sink onto. I moan when I push down, and the head slips in easily enough, then I hiss as he pushes past the tight ring of muscles.

"Oh, shit," I pant, leaning forward, resting my forehead on his shoulder.

Biting the muscle there, he hisses at the pain, then I lick and kiss the area. I sink all the way down his shaft, loving the feeling of being full of him.

His hands tighten on my waist, then they move down to my arse and spreading me wide as I ride him; rocking back and forth, then bouncing up and down. My dick rubs against his stomach, pre-cum wetting his skin.

My balls feel heavy, full, and ready to empty all over him, to mark him as he has done me. I fuck him, ride him into the bliss we are chasing. Looking down at him, I see he is watching me, his eyes dark with lust.

The look on his face causes my balls to tingle and draw up. I know I'm close, but I want to draw this out longer. I want Leo to come first.

Sitting up a little and reaching behind me, my hand trails over his thighs and down between his legs, over his balls, and down to his arsehole. My back arches as I reach the place I want, as I keep rocking my hips, fucking him. Adding pressure with circular motions against his tight hole, Leo howls as I push my finger into his arse.

Grinning at him, I push further in, and his eyes widen and darken at the same time, He braces his hands on my hips, holding me in place as he fucks up into me. I cry out his name, as he growls and grunts in furious passion.

Keeping my finger deeply in place, he angles himself so he is fucking my arse and finger at the same time. The feeling is overwhelming, as well as seeing this amount of passion come from him.

Over and over again he fucks me, taking me to new heights. Desire travels up my spine, and my balls fucking blow, shooting cum all over Leo's stomach and chest. Some even hits his chin.

"Yes. Fuck!" He comes seconds after me, filling me up.

My body feels boneless as I collapse against his chest, not caring about the cum between us. Sweat covers our bodies, but neither of us care. In fact, there is an intimacy to the way we are sitting.

"That was so bloody good," I grunt against his neck, before kissing the salty skin there.

Flicking out my tongue, I taste him, making him hiss. His hips buck up into me, and I let out another grunt at the full feeling.

"It's always good with you, baby. It was also a reminder of who you belong to." He cocks an eyebrow at me, which makes me grin. Kissing him one once more, I cup his jaw.

"I know who I belong to, but you can't stop me from having male friends, Leo. I don't say anything about you hanging around with a brother," I explain.

"That's different. None of them are gay. I don't want to fuck any of them." He shivers and I laugh at him.

"Not all my friends are gay, Leo. Yes, Wayne is gay, but he knows who I belong to, okay?" He looks at me for a beat and then nods, slapping my arse.

"Come on, I need to get you cleaned up so I can dirty you again."

"Why bother to wash then?" I question, sitting up and looking at him.

He cups my jaw, bringing me in for a kiss. His tongue devours my mouth, but the kiss is over before I can deepen it.

"Because I want to see you all wet and silky. Now move it, babe," he states, helping me off his lap and soft dick.

I wince as I climb off him, then follow him into the shower, and it's in there that he sucks me off, and I him. He washes every inch of my body, taking his time to savour the feel of me in there with him. In the shower, I never get Riot the SAA biker of the MC; I get Leo Peters, my boyfriend.

It's nice, different, and just what we need.

Twenty-Six

Riot

My blood is pumping through my veins, hot and hard. We tracked that cunt Harry down, and we found out he's been spreading a shit load of lies about Ben and the club. He told his friends that we beat him within an inch of his life because Ben was jealous that he had moved on. Fucking prick.

"Easy, Riot," Chaos warns as I shut my bike off, around the corner from the little rat's flat.

"Oh, easy comes to mind when I think of beating that little rat cunt. I'll beat the little snake, then leave. Easy-fucking-peasy, Prez," I snap.

We walk to the block of flats, not caring who sees us. Most fear us anyway, and the police are in our pockets so they will do fuck all. I nod to a druggy fuck that I collect money from, who also lives in the block. He was the one who gave me the heads up that the rat was home.

"Unlock the door," Psycho snaps at someone, standing close to the door, smoking a joint. The bloke rushes to type in a code and the door buzzes. He pulls the door open for us.

Not giving him a second glance, I rush through and up the single flight of stairs. Not waiting for my brothers to catch up with me, I raise my foot up and kick the door in. With one boot it springs open, the wooden frame splintering.

Girly screams come from the living room. Stomping through the small flat, I see Harry standing in front the couch in a pair of rainbow boxers and a fur coat, watching gay porn while smoking a joint. However, that isn't what freaks me out; it's the movement coming from inside said rainbow boxers.

"What the fuck is that?" Mayhem calls out from behind me, pointing at Harry's crotch.

Harry quickly reaches inside the material and pulls out a hamster, revealing what he had tucked down there. A gagging sound comes from behind me, and I look over my shoulder and see Keys retching. He holds his hand up to us, silently telling us not say a fucking word, but my anger for this cunt is more powerful than ribbing my brother.

"You sick fuck." I march forward and slam my fist into his jaw. "You need to stay the fuck away from Ben. He is mine." I hit him again and he falls to the floor.

He curls into a ball, cowering like the pussy he is, and tries to protect his head from the blows I rain down on him. I can hear shuffling behind me, but I don't stop. Gripping his neck, I pull his bloodied face close to mine, making sure he knows who he's fucking with.

"You will stay the fuck away from Ben. No more lies, no more threats via text or email. Fucking leave him alone. He has moved on to something better, obviously. You need to get that through your sick thick skull."

I throw him to the floor then kick him in the ribs for good measure, before walking out of the room. I can hear Mayhem adding some warning to the prick, but I've used enough energy on the fucker, so he gets no more of my time.

Lighting up a smoke, I wait for my brothers to join me so we can move onto the second part of our night. We got word from our people on the streets that the crew that beat Ben up for being gay are camped out near some old, abandoned swimming pool.

"How did you know it was him sending the texts, and who left a dead rat on his doorstep?" Mayhem asks as he lights his own smoke.

Taking a long drag, I blow the smoke out. "One of Ben's friends saw the images on Harry's phone and looked through it. He was sickened at the texts he had sent, so he contacted me," I explain in a flat tone.

Happy enough with the information, we stand in silence.

One by one, my brothers join me, and we have a quick smoke. People are watching us but they say nothing. The nicotine seeping into my lungs calms me, but I know it won't last long. My rage will boil over when we get to the cunts who hurt my old man.

"You ready for this?" Chaos asks. I nod, flicking my cigarette to the ground before using the sole of my boot to put it out.

"I'm always ready," I reply, while mounting my bike. They follow me and we wait for Prez to pull out.

We follow in formation. Even though it's my old man we're getting justice for, we still follow protocol. It takes us a good forty minutes to reach where the punks are hiding. We each park our bikes and hide them behind a rundown, brick bus stop; one like I used to use when I was a teenager.

"No going gung-ho, brother. We take it easy; make sure we get every motherfucking one of them," Mayhem states, his voice leaving no room for argument. Nodding, we all make our way around the building, each of my brothers taking up their positions.

Mayhem is with me, and Psycho is covering Prez—not that he needs it. Every member of the Road Wreckers MC hard motherfuckers. They know how to handle the law and they know how to handle themselves in a fight; fist, or gun.

Glass crunches under my boots. I shake my head and look to my brother, who smirks at me.

Looking up, we find an eight-foot-high window. Mayhem pulls himself up and looks through the busted glass.

"They look high as fuck, and the shitty rap music they're playing is enough to deafen an army. They clearly don't give a hit about security," he says, dropping to the ground. "Let's go." I nod, and we creep closer.

A fire exit door hanging off its hinges comes into view, and Mayhem slowly opens it. We sneak inside, making sure to keep our wits about us as we close in. My gun is raised, though I don't want to use it. I'm more inclined to use my bare hands to drain their lives away.

We peer through the next door and see six pricks, all smoking up a storm. They're laughing and joking; one is trying to rap but keeps slurring his words. They are all dressed in baggy tracksuits and baseballs caps—proper street thug looking, but I know they're fucking cowards because they never fight fair. Well, tonight they will know everything about being treated unfairly.

High or not, these fucks will feel my wrath.

Across the room, in another doorway, Chaos can just about be seen. As for everyone else, I don't need to see them to know they're in position.

Our president gives the nod, and we all move. I creep up behind an arsehole in his chair and rest my gun against his head. He freezes, and his friends freak out, but my brothers step into place, each of them training a gun on one of the boys.

"Boys, I see you've been busy. Throwing your weight around town. Bullying people for fun. Causing public damage. Well, tonight, fuckers, it ends." Chaos says firmly, in a low tone that's been known to scare people.

The boys' eyes go wide with fear, but of course they have a couple who think they are big boys. Shaking their shock off, they begin to mouth off.

"Fuck off, old man. We can handle you lot." The punk gets to his feet and pulls out a knife.

I look at Mayhem, and he smirks at me. Chaos outright laughs, and Psycho grins his maniacal smile. It's the kind of smile that belongs in a horror film.

"What the fuck?" one bitches. I aim my gun at him, and he freezes.

One of them cackles. "You bring guns because you can't take us on hand to hand."

Now I'm pissed.

"Says the punk with a knife. Drop it and let's go, fucker," I call out, placing my gun on one of the stacks of barrels lined up in front of the wall.

When I beckon to him with my fingers, he glares at me—and then charges. He throws a punch, and I lean back, dodging it. He keeps coming at me and I laugh at his shitty, weak attempt.

I hear the guys beating the crap out of the ones who came at them, then grunts, cries of pain, and skin hitting skin sounds throughout the room. I smile, knowing my brothers are handling the punks who are trying to be big men.

Psycho he has already knocked the two guys out and is leaning against the wall with a smoke in his mouth, watching us with a bored look on his face. The two guys at his feet are bloodied up to fuck. I can't tell if they're breathing or not. Knowing my brother, it's likely to be the latter.

While looking at him, the little shit takes advantage of my distraction, making his move. The pain in my arm tells me the cunt got me. Looking down at my arm, I see blood seeping through the material of my tee. Growling, I look at him, seeing his smirk, and now it's my turn to lunge and end this once and for all.

196

My hand grips his throat before he can even blink, and I tighten my fingers, stopping him from breathing. Stupid on my part.

I should have rid him of the knife first.

The cunt stabs me in the side, but I'm able to grip his wrist before he pushes it in further, causing more damage.

"End it, Riot. Stop toying with the prick," Chaos bellows.

I hiss at the pain and pull his hand back, removing the blade from my body. His arms tremble when I turn the blade on him—as I stab the cunt with his own knife, right in his shoulder. His eyes go wide with pain and fear, but I ignore it, pushing the blade in deeper. Blood oozes out of him, coving my hand and his.

I watch as his eyes blink, before they close completely, and he passes out from the fear, shock, and the blood loss. He will live, but he will have a reminder of tonight. He won't fuck with the Road Wreckers MC again.

"This is for my old man. The man you and your punk friends beat up a few weeks ago." I pull the knife out and plunge it back into his hand. "This is for all the pain and damages you've caused people."

I drop him to the floor.

This kid could have lived his life differently, but he decided to take the easy and cowardly way out. Stealing and hurting people to get what he wants. Fucking pigs, the lot of them. I may be a criminal, but I earn my money. I only hurt people who need to be hurt, never the innocent, and I never steal.

I feel a hand on my shoulder, and I turn my head to see Mayhem standing next to me. Like me, he's covered in blood and grime.

"Come on, man, we need to go. Keys will make sure nothing can be traced back to us." I look over at my brother and he nods, already spilling petrol over everything.

197

"Fuck, will Ben want to be with me when he sees me like this?" I ask no one in particular as we get to our bikes.

"Does Lizzie, Olivia and Evie support us after all the shit we've done?" I nod. "Brother, Ben loves you. He knows how the club works. He will support you no matter what. He will help lift you up when you're being a cunt, and he will clean you off," he adds, pointing to the blood covering me.

Looking down, I see blood is seeping into my cut, close to one of my patches. Shit.

"Ben will know what to do. He's a good man. I mean, he is my brother so of course he's awesome." Mayhem winks and mounts his bike.

I follow suit, giving my brother a chin lift before pulling away, leaving behind the scum that hurt Ben. Tonight should be a lifetime warning to them to take a new path, before they get hurt again, or worse.

Tonight solidifies everything I already knew. I love Ben, and tonight, I will tell him.

Twenty-seven

Ben

Placing Friday's bowl on the floor, she waits patiently for the command to eat. Smiling, I stroke her head. "Eat." She dives right in.

The smell of raw food took me a while to get used to, but now it doesn't bother me because I know how good it is for her.

I rinse out my plates from dinner and stack them in the dishwasher, just as the garage doors rise.

Frowning, I go to see if it's Riot or my brother. Neither told me they were coming here tonight because they had some club stuff to take care of. Pulling open the door that leads from the kitchen to the garage, I see Riot stiffly climb off his bike. Rushing to him, I suck in a breath when I see all the blood.

"Holy fuck. What happened?" I say to him, supporting his body.

We walk into the kitchen, my heart racing as I help him sit on one of the island stools.

"Talk to me, babe," I say to him, pulling the cut off his body and putting it on the counter, then moving to his t-shirt, which is saturated in blood.

Bringing his head up, he looks at me with tired eyes, but I see relief there. Is that from seeing me or something else?

"We tracked down the guys who beat you and dealt with them," he states. "Fuck." He winces as he shifts position.

I scan his body, clocking the slice on his arm, which seems to have stopped bleeding. Moving down, I see some bruises have already formed. Then I come to a wound just beneath his ribs. Shit.

Dropping to my knees, I inspect the injury. It doesn't look deep and is only about two inches wide. Blood trickles out of it slowly, but it looks like it's clotting.

"Baby, I like you on your knees," he jokes.

"Not the time, Leo, for fuck's sake. Let's move you to the upstairs bathroom. I need to get you in the shower to wash this blood off, then I need to patch you up," I state.

With one of his arms over my shoulder, I guide him upstairs and into my bathroom, then strip him down and turn the shower on. He hisses as the hot water runs over his naked body, while I strip out my own clothes. Looking down at the shower floor, I see the water turn red, then fade to pink as it slips down the drain.

What the hell happened tonight? I know he won't go into detail with me, and a part of me is okay with that. Whatever he and the club did, it was to protect me, and that's something I will forever be grateful for.

Using the shower gel, I lather up his body, getting all the sweat, grime and dry blood off him. Clearly not all the blood is his, because of the sheer amount of it doesn't match his injuries, looking at his two small wounds. I avoid getting soap in the wounds and clean him up, before moving on to his hair.

Looking at his face, I see his gaze fixed on me. His eyes are dark with lust, and my dick takes note of the desire there. We both stare at each other, no words needed to be spoken.

His dick bumps mine, drawing my attention away from his face.

Shit, he's as hard as I am.

"You can get on your knees. Make me feel better. I am hurt after all." he mutters. My head snaps up and I see him smirking at me.

"Arsehole," I mutter and climb out of the shower.

"Yeah, I can fuck you there too." Shaking my head at him, I wrap a towel around my waist and do the same for him while he stands there with a dark, intense look in his eyes.

Standing in front of this man with blood dripping from his arm, and a wound in his side, my heart stutters. All the feelings force their way forward, reminding me of what we have built over the years. How things have happened so fast over the last few weeks. How he's bleeding for me. Holy fuck.

"I love you." I blurt it out, but it feels right telling him. Will it be a killer if he rejects me? Hell yes. But I feel deep down that he won't. I feel that he feels the same way. I mean, he wouldn't hurt or kill people for someone he just cares for, but then again, he would for the club, for my brother.

He stares at me, saying nothing. Time ticks by and my stomach sinks into my bare feet. Taking a step back, I spin on my heel and rush into my bedroom, ready to get dressed and find a first aid kit. Maybe I should have done this before we showered. Shit.

Pulling on a pair of random shorts, I ignore his presence behind me. My heart is trying to break free from my chest, and my breathing has become choppy, but I try to hide it. I won't let him see how much his silence has hurt me.

"Ben," he says. I look over my shoulder and find him sitting on my bed, blood making the towel turn pink. I wince and rush out of the room.

"Be right back," I call out.

I head to the kitchen and grab the first-aid kit, then take a deep breath before going back upstairs. Riot is lying down on my bed, his legs dangling over the side, looking like a bleeding Greek god.

I clear my throat and step into the room. "Let me patch you up."

He lifts his head up, looking at me with intense eyes. He goes to sit up but I stop him.

"Stay. I can stitch this, and then do your arm." I keep my voice firm, not letting my pain show, but Riot has other ideas.

After sitting on the bed next to him, I start pulling items out of the box. His hand finds my wrist, halting my movement.

My gaze slides over to him, and I find him smiling at me, which makes me frown.

"Come here," he says, and I shake my head.

"No. I need to get this done to stop the bleeding." Ignoring the slight tug on my wrist, I snatch it back and get to work.

I add the numbing cream to his side first, then apply the butterfly strips to his arm, as there's only a shallow slash there. It doesn't take long. Once finished, I prepare to stitch his side up. Riot doesn't flinch; he just keeps his gaze on me. Hot and intense.

My body heats up from his attention, my cock responding even though my man is hurt and didn't say he loved me back. His hand trails over the outside of my thigh, making my skin tingle and my cock twitch.

Damn it.

"There, it's all done," I state, smoothing my finger across the small, rectangular bandage.

When I sit back, Riot jack-knifes up in the bed, taking my face in his hands and kissing the life out of me. Gasping for air, I pull back, expecting Riot to let my face go, but he doesn't. He only grips me tighter.

"I love you, Ben. Always have and always will. You're my ride or die, baby. You bolted while I was basking in the feeling of knowing a man like you, who is way out of my fucking league, loves me."

"Fuck," I mutter, and he laughs.

"Oh, we are definitely fucking, babe. Ride me." He lies back down, removing his towel.

Shaking my head at him, I rest my hand on his stomach.

"No, you're hurt."

"That's why you are going to do all the work, baby. I'm going to lie here and let you fuck me. Don't keep me waiting, Ben. I could have fucking died tonight, and the thought of never seeing you again is fucking with my head. I need to feel you, all of you, to know we are here and alive."

Bloody hell, when he puts it like that...

Quickly ridding my body of my shorts, I bend at the waist and take his cock into my mouth. He's hard, hot, and heavy against my tongues. Just how I like him. I suck on him, moving my mouth up and down his shift, my hand toying with his balls.

He groans and pants out my name as I pleasure him.

Bobbing up and down, I can feel he's close. My balls scream to empty, so I pull my mouth off, wanting to come with him. Reaching for the top drawer of my side table, I pull out a bottle of lube and apply some to my fingers before massaging it into my arsehole, getting it slick so he can slide in.

When I add some to his cock, Riot hisses at the coolness of the liquid.

"I want this to be fast and hard, babe," he tells me. "Fuck me, Ben."

I straddle his waist, keeping my weight off him completely. Lining up his cock, Riot aims right for my hole as

203

I lower myself down on him. We both hiss and growl out at the sensation. The overwhelming need to be connected.

I slide all the way down, still not putting my weight on him, and I know my calves will hate me tomorrow.

"Oh fuck, yeah, baby, fuck me." Using my strength, I slide up and down his cock, letting the pure euphoric feeling take over me.

His hands move under my arse, guiding me up and down as I fuck him. My cock bobs between us, hitting his stomach and leaving a trail of pre-cum on his skin.

My legs burn; my balls feel heavy.

Sweat covers our bodies.

Breathing harshly, we speak each other's names as we both chase the climax to end all climaxes.

Leaning forward, I brace my hands next to his head, keeping my gaze locked on his. The love shining through is beyond anything I ever expected from him. My knees hit the bed, and I rock back and forth, making sure not to jerk him too much.

"Oh, shit, yes," he growls as he slips in deeper, and it's then I know he likes me riding him like this.

"Fuck, I'm going to come," I groan, throwing my head back. His hand finds my cock, and he starts jerking me in time with my thrusts.

"Come—now," he bellows as I feel him come inside of me.

Pulse after pulse, he fills up my arse, just as my balls explode, shooting my cum over his chest and stomach.

"Oh fuck," I whimper, my body suddenly weak.

Not wanting to but knowing I need to, I climb off him, watching his soft cock flop out of me and onto his stomach, where my cum is sitting. Moving to lie next to him, Riot wraps his arm around me, cupping my jaw, angling my head up and kissing me.

The kiss is slow, sensual. Intense and loving.

"I love you, Ben Miller. You are my old man, and I am yours. One day you will marry me, I have no doubt, and I want to have a family with you."

His words shock me, but they make my heart sing.

"I love you too, Leo Peters. I will marry you any time, and you will be a cracking father to our kids. Adopt or surrogate, we will have a family. Just try not to come home covered in blood again," I state, grinning.

He smiles back at me. "Is that your way of asking me to move in with you, babe?"

Shaking my head. "No, that's my way of telling you you're moving in." I wink.

He chuckles and kisses me again, letting me know all is right in the world.

I'm ready for the *riot*that is going to be my life going forward.

205

Epilogue

Riot

Cigar in one hand and a glass of whisky in the other, I watch my club and my family laugh and piss about, enjoying the day. It has been six months since everything went down with the crew that beat Ben. Six months of having him in my life.

Today, we mark the milestone of Ben hitting a number of bestselling titles all over the world with his new dark MC series. He lightly based each of the books on a member of the club, adding in some extra killing and torture. His sex scenes are hot as fuck as well, so hot that they turned him on while writing while them, which in turn meant I got to benefit from the horniness he created. No wonder women around the world love my man's books. They get horny reading them, then they get to jump their men when they come home.

Win-win I say.

"He's lapping this shit up," Mayhem pipes up from his seat next to me.

Turning my head to look at him, I wear a proud smile on my face, because I am beyond fucking proud of my man.

"Fuck yeah he is. He deserves it. That series took months to write, each book becoming more in demand than the last. He took it in his stride and put out the best books he could."

Psycho smirks at me. "Evie has been reading them. Thanks for that, by the way."

"Hey, he writes damned good sex, believe me. Turns me the fuck on," I reply, and he tips his beer bottle at me.

The kids are playing, and the dogs are chilling in the shade. Everyone's happy and enjoying the day. Glancing over at my brothers, I see them watching their old ladies. Everyone is happy as fuck, and since things have been good round here for the last six months, we deserve some time to relax and enjoy some club time.

The night I got back from ending the crew and dealing with rat-faced Harry, something changed between Ben and me. The last piece slipped into place, connecting us for all motherfucking time. The way he tended to me without hesitation, without questions or judgment... He cleaned me up, fucked my brains out, and then held me while we slept.

Me, a fucking biker, was held by his old man, but I tell you what, I slept like a fucking baby. We woke up the next morning and Ben made love to me, slow and deep. Something I had never done before him. Then we showered, careful of my wounds, and made breakfast, both going through the motions like the violence of the night before never happened. That afternoon, I moved all my shit into his house, and I've been there ever since.

Everything snapped into place. Our connection became complete.

Looking across the yard, I see Ben sitting with the old ladies, chatting about the new series he plans on writing soon. He hasn't given me too much detail yet. He has notes all over the fucking office, so thank fuck I don't go in there much. But I do hear him muttering to himself from time to time, and then I know I have to nail him down and make him take a break.

Speaking of nailing him down…

Mayhem kicks my foot, and I turn to look at him. Smiling, he winks at me, and I know it's time. Their dad is sitting with us, and he gives me a nod, giving me the blessing to do what I am about to do.

Getting to my feet, I place my fingers in my mouth and whistle to get everyone's attention.

Everyone stops and looks at me. Friday barks, making me laugh, because that girl does not like being woken up.

"Ben, come here, babe." Frowning, he puts his drink down on the table and walks over to me. Pulling him to me, bring my lips to his, sealing our fates together in one kiss.

Not one to beat around the bush, I drop to my knees, and Ben's eyes go wide, but he smiles down at me.

"I'm not doing all that girly shit you read and watch on TV. I'm a fucking biker, and you love that about me, so I'm doing this biker style. You're my ride or die, Ben. I would die for you. I will be loyal to you. I will protect you. And most of all, I will love you."

I pull out the box that holds two black wedding bands.

"Men don't tend to wear engagement rings, so I went straight and bought us wedding bands. Yours has a thin red line in the middle, and mine is plain. Will you marry me, Ben Miller? Will you officially become my old man, property of Riot and husband of Leo Peters?"

Everyone waits on tenterhooks for his reply, but I know and trust my man. He drops to his knees, kissing me like there's no tomorrow. Gripping my face, he doesn't let go, even with everyone cheering and clapping around us. Our tongues duel in his mouth, teeth hitting, the kiss is that intense.

It only ends when a fluffy fucking mutt pushes between us. Friday is a fucking cock block, I'll tell you that now. She pushes her head between our faces, licking first Ben's and then my face. Little shit.

"Fuck off, Friday, you were licking Winston's balls just now."

Everyone laughs at her antics. Friday has a thing with Logan's dog, Winston.

"Like you don't lick Ben's balls," Keys calls out. I flip him off, smiling at the bastard.

"So, what's the answer, babe? Will you marry me?"

"Fuck yes, I will marry you." He pushes Friday to the side, which makes her whine, but Logan calls her, and she runs off.

I kiss my man again, but the club has other ideas. We're pulled to our feet and passed around, receiving hugs and slaps on back in congratulations.

My family, my club, and my old man accept me for exactly who I am. They don't judge; they do not demand.

When Ben became mine, I felt like a new *riot* was about to start, one we would ride together, side by side. Now that does sound like fun.

We are the Road Wreckers MC, and we live for the road, for our families, and for the club.

THE END

209

Acknowledgments

Again, I have to thank you, boss man, my King. Thank you for always supporting me and at my side through it all. I love you, baby.
My 3 babies, even though you aren't babies anymore. Always be you.
Thank you to my special editor, Steph for making Riot readable, and for shouting at me when needed.
To Dana, who made this cover HOT. Thank you.
To my Wreckers girls, Claire, Ruby and Ellie, you are stars, and it has been a pleasure working with you all.
And last but not least, because as the hashtag says #AlwaysLast. Thank you to the amazing readers for the support and kind words.

Books by author.

Standalones
Let Me Love You
What Are The Chances
This Time Around
Defeating The Odds
Christmas at Paradise Meadow

The Phoenix Boys
Rafe
Ryder
Reeve

Castle Ink
Dex
Jay
Ivy

Unforgiven Riders MC
Claiming Mine
Protecting Mine
Taking Mine
Getting Mine
Keeping Mine

Reckless Angels MC
Part 1 - Twisted Tales of Mayhem
Part 2 - Twisted Steel

Santa's Naughty Helpers – Unwrapping Mine
Twisted Steel Second Edition: NOMAD

Rebel Hype
Creed - Heart Beats Anthology

Rugged Skulls MC
Magnum
Opal
Slide
Sarge
Rookie
Edge

Rugged Ink
Zeb

About the author.

Amy lives in South Wales with her husband and 3 children. Their family dogs and musk turtle. Besides writing Amy is very fond of photography and a lover of music. She is also a big fan of Supernatural, Sons of Anarchy, plus The Medici. Amy is also a huge ice hockey fan, mainly the Cardiff Devils. She loves spending time with her family and friends, plus meeting new people. From bad boys to rock stars and bikers, Amy's books cover them all.

Media links.

Author Page
https://www.facebook.com/AmyDaviesBooks

Amy's Awesome Nerds- https://bit.ly/2krhglW

Goodreads:
https://www.goodreads.com/author/show/7255950.Amy_D
avies?from_search=true

Twitter: @AmyDaviesAuthor

Instagram: www.instagram.com/AmyDaviesBooks

Bookbub: https://www.bookbub.com/authors/amy_davies

Newsletter: http://eepurl.com/c4miz1

Amazon.co.uk: Amy Davies: Books, Biography, Blogs,
Audiobooks, Kindle

Printed in Great Britain
by Amazon